# THE HOUSE OF THE OCTOPUS

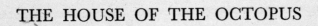

# THE HOUSE
# OF THE OCTOPUS

*By*

CHARLES WILLIAMS

LONDON
EDINBURGH HOUSE PRESS
2 EATON GATE, S.W.1
1945

*The fee for an amateur performance of this play is £3, 3s., and all enquiries should be addressed to the publishers, Edinburgh House Press.*

*First published* 1945

PRINTED IN GREAT BRITAIN BY
MORRISON AND GIBB LTD., LONDON AND EDINBURGH

# PREFACE

THIS play is not meant to have any direct topical relation. The name of P'o-l'u and the title of its Emperor were taken from certain earlier poems published before the outbreak of war. It is true that they were there referred to the sixth century, but it is unlikely that between the sixth and the twentieth centuries the state of P'o-l'u, within or without, has much changed; and I should regret now an identification with any particular nation or land which would then have been impossible. It is rather a spiritual threat than a mortal dominion.

Neither are the Chorus and its leaders meant to present any particular locality. Certain details of their original worship are taken from Mr John Layard's fascinating *Stone Men of Malakula*, but ' the Outer Seas ' is a sufficient place for them. It may be argued that these natives are too metaphysical. But the effort after simplicity in verse is likely to end in mere silliness; outside lyric, its achievement is on the whole the mark of the greatest poets in their greatest moments. Nor am I wholly convinced that such a simplicity would be any truer to these imagined minds than their present speech. Their hymn is a free translation from a twelfth century hymn to the Holy Spirit by St. Hildegarde.

The character of the Flame, or the *Lingua Coeli*, is meant to be exactly what he says : that energy which went to the creation and was at Pentecost (as it were) re-delivered in the manner of its own august covenant to the Christian Church. I had some idea that his dress might suggest this by being of a close flame-colour within and of a deep star-sprinkled blue without. When he speaks to the Christians he throws back his outer cloak; when to the others, he gathers

5

it round him. But this is only a suggestion which I do not press. No effort should, I think, be made to distinguish Alayu's appearance in the first two acts from that in the third.

It remains only for me to thank the United Council for Missionary Education for having asked me to write the play, and for their great kindness throughout. And I should like especially to thank Miss Margaret Sinclair, the convener of the Plays Group. It cannot often happen to an author to meet with such understanding of what an author's business is.

CHARLES WILLIAMS

# DRAMATIS PERSONÆ

LINGUA COELI, in the form of a Flame

ASSANTU

RAIS—his wife

ANTHONY—the missionary priest

SIRU—a deacon

TORNA—  
TANTULA } men of the land

OROYO—from a neighbouring island ; a man of the Chorus

ALAYU—a girl of the Chorus

THE CHORUS

THE IMPERIAL PREFECT

THE IMPERIAL MARSHAL

TWO SOLDIERS

*The scene is outside a newly built wooden church ; against it, a little higher than the roof, is a watcher's platform with a ladder. On the left and right of the church is the jungle, through which on the right a path leads to the village. Through a break at the back the sea can be seen. TORNA is on the platform.*

# ACT I

*It is full moonlight.* THE FLAME *comes out swiftly from the church, pauses, and speaks abruptly.*

### THE FLAME

Call this a land in the Outer Seas,
where the ease and joy of our Lord reaches at last ;
as in all the past of his Church, so now here.
First it was Jerusalem, then Damascus, Rome,
all the patriarchates ; and some of you to-night
are alive and alight with fire of this same kind.
O driven in search or dire in mastery, the mind
of God's Church is the only final subject of song.
It is the only and universal joy.
Joy is man's condition and our language.
We are of those who first came into being
when the Holy Ghost measured within the waters
the angle of creation ; then in a sudden visibility
we dropped from his rushing flame-scattering wind,
to teach the blessed the speech of heaven and of us.

### THE CHORUS (*within the church*)

Fire of the Spirit, life of the lives of creatures,
spiral of sanctity, bond of all natures,
glow of charity, light of clarity, taste
of sweetness to sinners, be with us and hear us.

### THE FLAME

But each among us has his own charge ; and I,

9

this new congregation of the faithful in a land
of the Outer Seas, brought to Christ's doom
by a missionary mouth.   Sins flooded away,
a stay of guilt granted for old faults
by the joyous equity of heaven, and food given—
well might they thrive !   But now see, how it happens
that an empire of paganry lies within these seas,
called P'o-l'u ; it has long stayed quiet,
but now moves.   It stretches wide tentacles,
gasps and clutches, and one by one fetches
into its maw these ancient scattered islands.
O now who shall save my young
innocent Church ? who but I ? and how I—
alas, you too know ; do you not ?
ask your hearts, my people, ask your hearts !—
heaven's kind of salvation, not at all to the mind
of any except the redeemed, and to theirs hardly.


THE CHORUS (*singing*)
Composer of all things, light of all the risen,
key of salvation, release from the dark prison,
hope of all unions, scope of chastities, joy
in the glory, strong honour, be with us and hear us.


THE FLAME
And—ask your hearts !—there are nearer dangers !
We who since Pentecost were granted by the Holy Ghost
to men's needs—we powers of heaven, we flames of the Spirit,
we seeds of conjunction—are sometimes seen on earth
in uncovenanted shapes, shapes of triumph and terror,
tempting gloom and greed.   Ask your hearts, my people,
if you do not mistake your desires for the fires of the Spirit :
mistake, did I say ?   God send that that be all,
that you do not crawl in a voluntary and besought error ;
terror indeed !   But here, on this wild shore,
a sorcerer's child has seen me so in the jungle,

and clairvoyantly traces my glow among the trees
by the sea's edge nearest P'o-l'u.   He long,
purposing to gain special and spiritual power,
pretended to keep the Faith.   That fails ;
he rails upon it and joins himself to my foes.
Now under the moon he comes again
hoping to catch me uncovenanted.   I will fill
his heart with me in his manner, be sure.   As I will
yours, if you choose ; as you wanted, if you insist.

> [*He begins to move among the trees.*   ASSANTU
> *enters slowly.*

### ASSANTU

Stay a little ! stay a little ! stay !
Stay for me, Flame of the dreadful Father !
You are he, I know, of whom my master
taught me, who go faster than a wind or a wave
and less traceable, in sea and air, than either,
and neither so strange nor so full of death as you.
O you, the dream and dance of feet more fleet
than theirs who beat the sand when the band of initiates,
in the old days when our people were still pious,
span in the house of spirits, below the heads,
smoke-dried and yoke-fitted, of our enemies
that hang under the beams.   Spirit, stay ;
they did not see you, Fire, but I saw you ;
in the angry smoke of the lodge of initiation
I called to you, fire of the lodge, fire of the spirit,
fire of the dead, licking and pricking our hearts
with the hunger of the sea, and the sea beyond the sea.
I only adore you, I alone of all our people.

### THE FLAME (*over his shoulder*)

I have told you before, you will not catch me thus.
Another latch than that of your lodge of initiates
opens upon us of heaven.   I have told you before

there is under all heaven one place only
where I am sworn to stay.   Go back ; go back.


ASSANTU

You look over your shoulder and seem to speak
but my hearing is too weak to catch your words.
The wind in the leaves and the waves on the shore deafen me.
They are mild, but their terrible mildness fills my ears
as if I felt the air of that shore
where the Father and Eater watches and waits for the dead.


THE FLAME (*dancing*)

Go back, Assantu, go back ; turn again.
Do you think I am here ?  I am not here ;  I am there
in the church with the holy ones.   What you can see here
is only a spark of the furious dance we made
before my companions and I were gathered and thrown
and sealed to the Christian altars and the souls of men.
It is your nature you see, Assantu, not me.


ASSANTU

The moon's rising is not more fixed than I
to pry after you in the jungle night by night.
I am one of the wise souls ;  turn and speak ;
speak loud ;  there is none as proud as I to hear.


THE FLAME

I speak to the proud only in their own tongue ;
there I am loud ;  otherwhere very soft,
whether in heaven, at the altar, or in the heart.
I am more gentle and cleansing than any water
for those who find fire in water and water in fire.


ASSANTU

I see an edge of you among the trees ;  my heart
seems to hear you ;  speak : what shall I do ?

## THE FLAME
Lay spells on the shining drops that are flung from the spray,
or the sparks that ride in the smoke.

## ASSANTU
I hear ! I hear !

That I can do.

## THE FLAME
Bid the shark swim

to be harmlessly stroked by your girls.

## ASSANTU
That I can do.

## THE FLAME
Command the dead heads in your lodge of spirits,
the tiny smoked heads of dead foes,
to swell where they hang from the roof and live and speak,
and shout as they once shouted when their dusty hands
clanged their spears together.

## ASSANTU
That I have done.

## THE FLAME
Go up to the images that stand along the cliffs
looking, for ever and ever, out to the sea—
as old men's stony longings gaze
out on the ways of the ocean they fish no more—
and bid them melt into manhood, and bring you safe
past the great shore of the ghostly island
where your fabled Father eats the fabled flesh.

## ASSANTU
That you must teach me.   I cannot do it.

## The Flame

If you could do all, you were no nearer me.
I tell you again there is no place but one
where the air that we—I and my fellows—breathe
is tolerable to mortal lungs, the tongues that we use
are audible to mortal ears. The chosen of my Lord,
the holy ones, are praying in the church ; go there.
There alone are my own, there alone.

*[He hides himself.*

## Assantu

I thought I heard you ; now I hear no more,
and the fire's edge is vanished. Spirit, stay ;
bring me to the other shore, bring me safe
past the Father who makes his meat of the dead
among the fiery volcanoes in the waste of the seas.
Save me from the soul's swallowing, O spirit, O fire !

## The Flame

I am weary of you, Assantu ; this very night
I am plight to my lord to begin the purging of souls.
Hark ! you hear the sea on the shore ; can you hear
the waves whispering about the transports of P'o-l'u ?
Hark ! you have another thought in mind,
designed to find without me the way of your will.
I will warn you no more ; go on, Assantu, go on.
The voice of your wife is near ; do your choice.
I shall see you again presently among the blesséd.

*[He goes into the church.*

## Assantu

Voice's echo and fire's edge disappear.
I hear a human foot.

*[He whirls round.* RAIS *enters.*

Ha, Rais !

Why do you follow me so ?

14

RAIS

Why do you go ?
Why do you wander from our hut night by night ?

ASSANTU
To know if that whose passage I saw in the jungle
will come out of the jungle.

RAIS

Twelve nights
you have gone thus, husband, under the moon.

ASSANTU
These nights, till the full of the moon, are thick
with the spirits of jungle, sea and sky.   Go.
You are my wife, but a woman : back to bed !
It is dangerous for women to walk in the full moon.

RAIS
Some—but I am the daughter of a wise woman,
and you, husband, less in that learning than she.
When I was a girl, I was not made a woman
with the other maids, but with a hidden rite
before the sacred images—more than yours.
For the sake of that, and being your wife, I come.

ASSANTU
Speak softly, lest the watcher above hear.

RAIS
Why does he watch ?

ASSANTU
To catch, in sea or sky,
sight of the flight of the planes or the sides of the ships
of P'o-l'u—P'o-l'u, the thick-tentacled octopus,
the empire of mastery within the waters.

15

RAIS

And you?

do you too wait here for P'o-l'u?

ASSANTU

Perhaps.

RAIS

You are a Christian.

ASSANTU

Am I? or am I not?

RAIS

You have been washed with their sacred waters; you have fed,
as I will never do, of their sacrosanct meal.

ASSANTU

I have known many rites. Do not you forget,
for all your talk of magic and your wise mother,
it was your brother who brought, ten years since,
in his own boat the white priest here.
You are the twin of a Christian.

RAIS

It was my shame

then, as now to be a Christian's wife,
if you are a Christian.

ASSANTU

Their meal is strong magic—
unearthly, but then I myself am half unearthly,
and I find in them and their meal no more than I have
in my own power already. Speak lower;
do not disturb our watchman lest his gaze
wander, and he do not see in the moon yonder
the thickening shapes of the ships when P'o-l'u comes.

16

## RAIS

What do you want ? do you want P'o-l'u to come ?

## ASSANTU

Yes, for then the white priest will flee.
He will go into the mountains and so hide
in a secret place, known only to a few
and there give counsel and care to all his churches.
It is so determined, and your brother to be his guide,
your brother Tantula who knows the enskied paths
between the heights.

## RAIS

If he does this, Assantu,
though he is my brother and of one birth with me,
I will call the curse of my mother on him.

## ASSANTU

No.

Save your breath to ask help of your mother
when you meet her after death in the ninth wave
of the spectral tide that beats then on this shore.
She will come dimly, floating and fleering on the waters.
You know that women do not find canoes
for their spirits, as men do, and never come
to the island where the Father eats men's flesh,
nor have hope of being made eaters themselves.
Yet—if you will go with me in this,
I might take you with me to feel the melting of the images
and come so to what safety lies beyond—
if you are no Christian.

## RAIS

I—Christian !

I !

## ASSANTU

Hush ! I have spoken with P'o-l'u.

RAIS

Husband !

ASSANTU

Hush !   I had a strange thought.   If . . .
if we could purge the land of all Christians—
and stand in the hut of initiates, the house of spirits !—
If the price were the sacrifice of your brother to-night ?

RAIS

I never had a brother since he was a Christian.

ASSANTU

P'o-l'u has its eyes and ears here ;
its mouth too.   I have spoken with it in the jungle.
It spewed me a token ;  look !

[*He holds something up in his hand.*

RAIS

The knotted octopus !
[*She falls to the ground.*

ASSANTU

P'o-l'u has great magic to give ;  it knows
the language the carved images speak.   Now
do you believe that I am greater than you ?

RAIS

Lord, my husband, have mercy on me !

THE CHORUS (*within*)

Amen.

ASSANTU

They will be coming presently.   Hark, you !
I and not your brother must be his guide ;
therefore your brother must have died.   Do you see ?

18

### RAIS

                              Lord,
say what you will have.

### ASSANTU

                            Stay you here,
hidden among the leaves.   If I sign—
throwing my hand up : thus—come you out ;
show yourself ;  call your brother for a last farewell ;
draw him aside here for one embrace.
Hold his arms.

### RAIS
Yes, lord.

### ASSANTU

                            I have said
I will betray the white man into their hands.
Do you understand ?

### RAIS
Yes, lord.

### ASSANTU

                            I had thought
to follow into the mountains and strike there.
This, if it may be, is better.   If I speak,
if I strike, obey.   If not, despair
at the parting a little, and presently let him go.

### RAIS
Yes, lord.

### ASSANTU
When they have the priest, the land
shall soon be swept of Christians, and the moon see

19

the house of spirits opened again, and the faces
of the images on the cliffs flicker with fire.
For this deed you and I shall live long
and when we die come speedily and safe
past the tides of the dead and the Ever-hungry
Father of ghosts.   P'o-l'u comes to-night.
Rise.   Will you spend your brother ?

RAIS

I am all yours.

ASSANTU

Go ; wait ; watch.   Now . . . Go.

[*She retires.*

TORNA

Who is there ?   Is that you, Assantu ?

ASSANTU
Yes ;
I myself.   I am late because my wife
wept paganly, and I would go christianly.
But we have forgiven each other.   Have you seen anything ?

TORNA

Nothing.

ASSANTU

Nor heard anything ?

TORNA

Nothing.

ASSANTU

Well,
it is likely the priest will not go to-night.

20

TORNA

He thinks, at dawn. Will you now go in?

ANTHONY (*within*)

. . . and of the Holy Ghost, be with you now and for ever-
more.

THE CHORUS (*within*)

Amen.

ASSANTU

They have finished; it is too late.

TORNA

Amen; amen.
Blessed be Jesus Christ, true God and true Man.
[THE CHORUS *begin to come out of the church;*
TANTULA, SIRU *and* ANTHONY *last.*

SIRU

Will you not consider, sir, and go now?

ANTHONY

No, son; let me stay to-night.
To-morrow in early light we will offer the Sacrifice
once more. Till we can see their ships from the shore
I need not think of flight. Tantula, tell me,
can we not reach the mountains in three hours?

TANTULA

The hills indeed, but a day more before
the heights, and as long again to reach a pass.
P'o-l'u may bomb the roads; it were wise to go.

ANTHONY

It is much against my will to go at all.

21

## ASSANTU

O sir, we have talked that out ;
do not let us trouble to talk more.


## ANTHONY

You were not with us to-night, Assantu.


## ASSANTU

No.

I had more charity for my wife than general charity.


## ANTHONY

Parity of love between the single and the whole
is a test of the soul's proportion in grace.    I
have for all and each of you an equal love,
being in my place but one equal among many . . .
however my place has been appointed chief.


## ASSANTU

If for our Father's sake we are willing to lack
your place and direction, do you take the track
and leave us to our Father.   He shall direct our lives.


## OROYO

Indeed it is too late now for anything else.
This afternoon I saw a single plane
flying westerly ; if they do here as elsewhere—
as in my own island—they will drop men
from many planes.   Hurry, sir, now.


## ANTHONY

I think you persuaded me against my own choice.


## SIRU

Sir, it is necessary that you should live
to give still, by God's will, direction to these isles,
and support between sea and sea the young Churches.

## ANTHONY

And I to live, and you perhaps die !

## SIRU

Sir, it is the privilege of the Church under God
in the light of the Spirit—and so we prayed and believed—
to decide who shall live and who die.
Have we not all died once ? this
was once your word and now you must obey your word.
This smallness of death is only an incident
in the new life ; which, since you brought us, we say
we must have you away to protect in elect hearts.

## TORNA (*from above*)

Sir, go ; if we may and as we may
we will let our brothers within the mountains know
how here it fares with us.  Go ; take our blessing,
and leave your blessing with us.

## ANTHONY

                        How can I go ?
It is not only my own heart's longings
that grieve to leave you—something of fear too.
Forgive the fear : let me speak my doubt out.
I have worked for you, my children, these ten years
with hopes and rejoicings—a small service to Christ,
to whom I, priced at nothing, might show
these pearls—earnest of the debt I ever owe.
Now, if I go, if I leave you to that enemy
P'o-l'u, how shall I endure the pains you bear—
the devastation and desolation of heart,
the physical agony, the extreme swallowing of death ?
Or how you indeed ?—and now I come
to my soul's inward trouble ; you are but young
in faith ; barely has the tongue of the Holy Ghost
           [THE FLAME *appears at the door of the church.*

23

uttered your names to Christ or his white dove
touched you with its wings ; is it sure of you ?   When
Christ wept in Gethsemane, it were hideous if then
it were for your apostasy his tears fell !
Hell is so easy.   You, by the shining waters
cleansed, then in the shining winds confirmed—
yes, and you, my son Siru, ordained !—
you are children still ; your very sins are childish,
unadult.   If now an adult evil—

THE FLAME

O peace, peace ! there are no adult evils.
Devils can never mature : only our Lord
grew and knew more.   Mystery of perfection,
to make a way to grow even in itself !

ANTHONY

—could you be faithful ? could you cling to election ?
could you be true ?   If I should go now,
would you swear again, each of you, to hold to his vow ?
You, Alayu, our youngest, would you swear ?

ALAYU

I ? why, yes, of course.

ANTHONY

Child, are you sure ?

ALAYU

O sir, Siru and you taught me love.
And could I ever deny that warm love ?
It is so much everywhere on the point of taking form,
to be more sweet than the promise—and that is sweet;
I could never deny the heat and hope of that love.

ANTHONY

Without help ! yet so you all say.

24

THE CHORUS (*softly*)

We are nothing ; yet by God's grace we are a few
new-called.   You brought us Christ, and we
in a host of confessors will bring you the Holy Ghost,
if God so please.   Do you doubt, father,
that you leave us, everywhere and always, with God Almighty?


THE FLAME

And they say his fatherhood is more efficient than yours.


ANTHONY

But to dare all these creatures of sea and air
that populate with hate and greed the spiritual world :
the log that within the marshes of a stagnant soul
becomes the crocodile ; the shark's tooth that tears
the despairing heart ; the negligent body caught
by waving tentacles ! the hidden dark surprise
of all the eyed creatures with meaningless eyes !
Can you, children, meet so mighty a test
from which, again and again, the best have quailed ?
If you must, can you die as I would have you ?
Speak in the Holy Ghost your inmost thought !


THE FLAME

Speak then ; being yoked ever to my own,
when I am invoked, I am always at once there.


SIRU

Sir, when in the disaster of paganry
we lay blind, you came to be our master ;
you gathered and fathered us ; now we are new-born :
little, but you told us the angels of little ones see
the face of the Father—


THE FLAME

And I tell you so too.

What is due to you and God we shall well pay,
if we may : do not fear ; you being gone,
we will walk alone ; his work must be done in us,
thus, or in some other way : and this
shall not be much amiss.  We must be ourselves
to him, if the time comes, and not you.
Young as we are, we shall do as God will have us,
if God give us grace : we must leave it at that.

The Chorus (*softly*)
We take refuge in the Maker of all and the Flesh-Taker ;
we believe that his deeds are enough for our needs ;
we believe that we are in him and he is in us.
Leave us thus, father, and go with God.

The Flame
Do quickly, Assantu, what you do.

Assantu
Do but go ; there is no time to spare,
and you and we will fare as well as we may.
Let Tantula but say a word at parting
to his sister my wife ; and rid yourself of delay.

Torna (*calling*)
Siru, Siru, I see shapes on the sea.

Assantu
It is they !

[Siru *runs up the ladder*.

Siru
Where ?

Torna
There !  over there !  see !

26

SIRU

Yes.   How many do you guess at ?

TORNA

Nine . . . eleven.

I think, eleven.

SIRU

I think, eight transports . . .
those in line, and an escort of three.   Small
ships all—a matter of three thousand men—
but more than needs for us.

TORNA

The whole foreshore,
the possible harbours, the passes behind ;  besides,
they may settle here the central garrison of the group.

SIRU

How long ?

TORNA

Two hours ; a little more than two hours.
They mean to be ashore before the setting of the moon.

SIRU

No planes.

TORNA

No planes yet.

SIRU

It is certainly they—
P'o-l'u in force.   They have a quiet sea ;
God give us calm minds to meet them.

[SIRU *and* TORNA *come down.*

SIRU

Now, father : you have here what you need ?


ANTHONY

In the sacristy, and the bread and wine in the church.


SIRU

We will go and fetch it ; let us all go—
one last moment of exchanged blessings,
then you on your way and we to wait in our homes.
Are you, too, ready, Tantula ?


TANTULA
Yes.
[*As they turn towards the church,* ASSANTU *throws
up his arm.* RAIS *comes out.*


RAIS

Tantula !

Brother !


SIRU
Who is that ?


ASSANTU
Who is that ?  Rais ! . . . My wife.
Why are you here ? we have not any time for you.


RAIS

I had a dream.   I saw my brother go,
and ran here to say good-bye.   One kiss,
Tantula !   I am your sister—though no Christian.


TANTULA
Fetch what is to be fetched.   Mine is over there.
I shall be ready to start by the time you are back.

28

THE FLAME

More than ready ; gone ; gone far.

SIRU

Well . . . come, father. But the bare time !

THE FLAME

The bare time is always and everywhere.
It is all there is, and so much all that all
is in it, everywhere and always. There is only Now
—the accepted time or it may be the unaccepted.

      [SIRU, ANTHONY, *and* THE CHORUS *have gone into*
         *the church ; he follows.*

ASSANTU (*to* RAIS)

Get him as far as you can among the trees.

ASSANTU (*to* TANTULA)

I will fetch your own bundle for you. Where ?

TANTULA

There—in the cloven tamarisk tree.

ASSANTU

                  Good.
I will be back as soon as they come. Wife,
when you have taken your parting, go to our house.

RAIS

Yes, husband.

            [ASSANTU *goes among the trees.*
      Must you go, Tantula ?

TANTULA

Yes.

### RAIS

Must *you* help this Christian teacher
to escape ? you, our mother's son ? might you
not fear our mother's vengeance—even here ?

### TANTULA

I was as much our mother's child as you.
But I have found the Father : I have come now
out of all these tales of a spectral Father
on his island which the smoke of many volcanoes veils,
but beyond them it lies in a spectral light, and he walks
horrid, gigantic, among spectral flesh
rotting round him till he makes his choice to eat
and the poor souls flying in the deadly air
everywhere, to be themselves swallowed and disgorged—
nightmare !

### RAIS

Salvation—

### TANTULA

Yes, indeed salvation
for those who drive before them bulls or swine,
dead also, to be eaten ghostly instead !
But now we know that the Father is a true power
of good, and his Son our food and not we his,
and there is but one Ghost, and that holy.
Think, sister, of this God. All the others
are nothing.

### RAIS

I will think rather of you now
than of any father : how can I other,
brother, when you are going on a difficult journey,
and the flowing of love between us must be staunched ?
You will not return.

TANTULA

We shall see that.   P'o-l'u
may not always be the proprietor of these isles,
and Christ is master of all.


RAIS

O your Christ !
Is he faster than the shark or more tentacled than the octopus ?
Come deeper.   I would not have your friends
watch a pagan weep at parting from her brother.
Yes ; you will go much farther than P'o-l'u.


TANTULA

If they have not closed the passes.


RAIS

If you should die,
you will have no boar or fat bull
to drive before you along the solitary road
where the dead come dreadfully to the bleak shore
and find an oarless canoe, and drift alone
to disembark—and you without a sacrifice—
on the other shore beyond, where the Father roams
amid putrid flesh and souls chirruping with terror.
Ask me, Tantula, to name a boar for you
that it may there choke and stifle and decay
instead of you.


TANTULA

This is all nothing.
We who have come to our Lord have only to go
farther with our Lord.   Everything that can happen
is only to go a little farther with our Lord.


RAIS

Where will you sleep to-night ?

TANTULA

As high as we may,
but briefly.

RAIS

Yes, briefly.   You will soon wake
to find yourself on the road.

[ASSANTU *re-enters behind.*

Hold me.   I will fold
my arms about yours.   Since I was a child
I have never held any but my husband so close.
Good repose to-night, my brother Tantula.
Whatever Father you find in the land of spirits,
you will find him quickly.   To-morrow I will kill a boar
in case his spectre may help you on the dolorous way.
Kiss me.

[*They embrace.   As* TANTULA *raises his head,*
ASSANTU *springs on him, strangling him.*


ASSANTU

Drag his arms down !

[*They disappear in the struggle.*


RAIS (*without*)

Is he dead ?


ASSANTU (*without*)

Finished.   Under the trees ; quick.

[SIRU *enters from the church.*


SIRU

Tantula ! . . . It is time now . . . Tantula !

[ANTHONY *and* THE CHORUS *re-enter.*


ANTHONY

Is my guide as ready as I ?

SIRU

He is not here.

ALAYU

He is saying good-bye to his sister among the trees.

OROYO

It is no time to linger over good-byes.
Where is he?

SIRU

Tantula!

TORNA

He is always an exact man.

Tantula!

SIRU

Can he have gone with Rais to her hut?
Up, Torna; look from the platform down the paths.

[TORNA *runs up*.

Well?

TORNA

I cannot see him.

SIRU

What of the fleet?

TORNA

The ships are clearer and closer. P'o-l'u comes.
No time to spare! Father, you must go, you must go!

[*He comes down*.

ANTHONY

Yes, but I cannot of myself reach the pass
without a guide.

SIRU

Who now? which of us knows?

[THE CHORUS *murmur dispersedly*.

TORNA

The foothills, yes; but not the upper roads.

SIRU

Torna, you had better go as far as you can,
and then do as you may.   God is over all,
and as much of the way as the wisest of us knows
is as far as he chooses we shall go of our own sight.
The rest he reserves.

TORNA

Assantu !  where is Assantu ?
Fool I was to forget ;  he could serve as well.
He can smell the roads almost as surely as Tantula.
Where is Assantu ?

SIRU

He gone too !

OROYO

Something evil is on us.

SIRU

You must not wait.
I perhaps know more than Torna.
I will come myself.

ANTHONY

No indeed, Siru.

TORNA

Assantu, Assantu !

ASSANTU (*coming in quickly*)

Here.   Quiet, all of you.

[*He seems to listen.*

P'o-l'u has landed spies here already,
scattered on the paths :  one we met.   Tantula
is dead by him—and he by me.   Rais
is safe in the village by now, I hope.   Enough.
No time for questions.

34

SIRU

Assantu—

ASSANTU

I heard as I came.

It is true ; I know the roads.

[*He listens.*

Maybe but one,
or maybe the rest have gone to the lower beaches.
I will go, father, if you will trust yourself to me.
I think the spies have not yet climbed as high ;
let us at least try.   Are you ready ?   And I.
What do you say, Siru ?

SIRU

I say, begone.

ANTHONY

Farewell then, and God have you in his keeping.

SIRU

Sleeping or waking, God keep you for ever.
Farewell.

THE CHORUS

We, confessing the only glorious Name,
we who have died once bid you a blessing ;
move where we may, there is only his joy in his giving,
and living or dying we go all in his love.

[ANTHONY *and* ASSANTU *go out.*

OROYO

It is strange, Siru, that there should have been no cry,
that a double death, so near, should be so mute.

SIRU

Why ? what do you mean ?

OROYO
I do not know.
If there were another guide . . . there is not.   Well,
God grant all go right.


THE FLAME (*from the church*)
That, Oroyo,
is the only thing past praying for.   Prayer
is only that you may enjoy things going all right.
Allow that, and see how simple prayer is.


SIRU
Back to the village now and wait for P'o-l'u.


ALAYU (*as the others go out*)
Siru !
SIRU
Yes ?
ALAYU
They will not hurt us very much,
will they ?
SIRU
Fear will hurt you much more.


ALAYU
I should not mind being hurt friendly, nor to die
without hurt, but . . .


SIRU
Think that our Lord
saw his enemies as his best and fairest friends
coming to do what he could not do for himself,
even he ; that is, to die at the will of another,
and could not help loving them for that kindness.
Come and try ; it is harder to think than to do ;  come.
[*They go out.*

## ACT II

*Day.* THE PREFECT *enters, with a soldier of P'o-l'u.*

### THE PREFECT

This is their temple, is it ?   Drive them up.
> [*The* SOLDIER *salutes and goes out.   He returns with
> another, driving in* THE CHORUS *singing.*

### THE PREFECT

Stop.   You are Christians, are you ?

### SIRU

Yes, lord.

### THE PREFECT

All of you ?

### THE CHORUS (*murmuring*)

Yes . . . yes . . . yes.

### THE PREFECT

In P'o-l'u we destroy Christians : you know that ?

### SIRU

Yes, lord.

### THE PREFECT

P'o-l'u is as empty of Christians
as the sea of pity or the hard rock of compassion
or the carved images yonder of springing rice.
What are those images ?

SIRU

They were made so long ago
that our people's earliest tales do not recall
how or when ; they were meant for likenesses of gods
worshipped once ; perhaps before men were born.


THE PREFECT

There are not and never were gods in P'o-l'u.
Only huger and hungrier cephalopods—which you
call octopuses ; over them and us and all,
in a hall quite empty of men and things,
the infinite nameless Emperor broods.  You may choose
between Emperor and cephalopods ; it is all you can.
It is all any man can who is caught by P'o-l'u.
You will only be quietly asked which you will choose,
but there are ways of asking.   So you are Christians.

[*He begins to walk down the line.*

Are you ?                                    (*abruptly to* SIRU).


SIRU
Yes, lord.


THE PREFECT

M'm.  Are you ?
(*to* OROYO)

OROYO

Yes.

THE PREFECT (*striking him*)
Speak courteously, pig.


SIRU

For Christ, Oroyo !

38

OROYO

Yes, lord.


THE PREFECT

Again.


OROYO

Yes, lord.


THE PREFECT

So.   And you ? (*to* TORNA)


TORNA

Yes, lord.


THE PREFECT

Why ?

TORNA

I was once a sinner—


THE PREFECT

What do you mean—' sinner ' ?
Do I know your foolish outlandish words ?
Talk intelligibly : what *is* sin ?


TORNA

What, unless one is careful, one forgets,
because, if one does not forget it, it is unbearable :
a weight in the heart, a misery ;  all the wrong—
yes, and along with it all the good—one has done,
run into nothing but a perpetual grief ;
no hope, no pause, no relief ;  then one becomes
dumb and blind and sick, and still goes on.
And then it is no longer so.

39

THE PREFECT

What do you mean ?


TORNA

Lord, I cannot say it ; I am a fool.
It is simply not so.   O for oneself,
one may be again lost in misery and pain ;
one may be stupid or wicked . . . it is not oneself
that matters ; it is this.   All that goes amiss
cannot at all alter that sweetness of fact.


THE PREFECT

What has this nonsense to do with your Christ-myth ?


TORNA

But that—that not so—that *is* Christ ;
and Christ is simply the denial of all one was ;
he bids let it pass ; sorrow perhaps he may allow
for oneself : but still, somewhere and somehow,
for someone—no, for everyone—he is quite certain :
in good and evil, in flesh and soul, not so.
That is our Saviour.   I know ; how can I deny ?


THE PREFECT

Many gods vanish in the wrappings of the cephalopods.
There is only one salvation then that counts,
and that is unreachable.   You will be free to say
on that day, if you can : *This is the not so.*
And you ? (*to* ALAYU) are you a Christian ?


ALAYU (*trembling*)
Yes.
40

## THE PREFECT

Yes ?

You mean you prefer the not so of the octopus ?

## ALAYU

Yes . . . No ; no.  I never was,
never.  O let me go !  It is all wrong—
I never did believe ; I can't believe . . .
I will believe anything you say I should.
Save me !  I will be the lowest slave of P'o-l'u !
Save me from the octopus !

## THE PREFECT

P'o-l'u does not want you.
If you are not a Christian, why are you here ?

## ALAYU

Because Siru talked to me about love,
and I thought love was coming to me in the drink
after the blessings.  They said Christ was love,
and I thought love was swimming into my blood.
I did not believe anything at all—only
I was lonely, and this was thrilling.  I was a fool.

## SIRU

Alayu—

[THE PREFECT *makes a gesture of silence.*

## ALAYU

I was willing and the old man talked.
I will love P'o-l'u.

### THE PREFECT

P'o-l'u does not want love.
My soldiers sometimes are glad of a woman or so.
That is all the love I can offer.   Will you go
to my soldiers or the octopus ?

### ALAYU

Anything, anything but that !
I swear I will never speak of love again.
Only save me !   I must not die so ;
I must not die yet.

### THE PREFECT

Must you not ?   I think
you must finish what you began.   If one man
possessed you, the rest would be hungry and jealous.
Besides, a man has only two arms.
An octopus, eight.   No ; it is too late.
You are officially a Christian.

### ALAYU

No, no !
[*She flings herself on her knees before him, clutching at
his waist.   A* SOLDIER *strikes her away with his
rifle.   She falls.*

### THE PREFECT

Dolt !   Have you killed her ?

### THE SOLDIER (*examining her*)

Yes, lord.

THE PREFECT

Fool !

First you are over-slow and then over-clumsy.
You should know your duties better.   For what it was worth
I would not have had her die before her time.
Report yourself for double guard duty
until I remember you—the later the better for you.
You are sure she is dead ?

THE SOLDIER
Yes, lord.

THE PREFECT

Accursèd fool !
[THE MARSHAL *enters*.

THE MARSHAL (*lightly*)

Dead ?

THE SOLDIER
Yes, Excellency.

THE MARSHAL

Ah well !

A Christian ?

THE SOLDIER
Yes, Excellency.

THE MARSHAL

A pity ! a pity !

These witty dialogues of yours, Prefect,
embarrass us all.   I call on you others to note
that this was against my personal command.   The body
shall be put at her co-religionists' disposal.
Meanwhile perhaps, to avoid more difficulty,

43

you will go, where I sent you, into the church.
I meant peace, and I hope we may have peace.


SIRU

May we carry the girl's body with us, lord ?


THE MARSHAL

By all means.   Whatever sacrifices are right
offer on my behalf.
>[SIRU *and* TORNA *take up the body, and carry it into
the church.*   THE CHORUS *follow.*


THE MARSHAL
You two, go with them.

*(to the* SOLDIERS*).*

They may talk, or sing—quietly—or do what they choose,
so long as you do not lose any of them.   Go.
They are all to stay there till I send orders.
>[*The* SOLDIERS *go into the church.*
I suppose your examination broke her down ?


THE PREFECT
I asked her if she was a Christian.


THE MARSHAL
I know ; I know.
You tasked her imagination too highly.
These revival religions are generally thick
with hysterical adolescents.


THE PREFECT
But, Excellency,
sooner or later you will put them all to death,
as your orders are ?

44

THE MARSHAL

My dear Prefect, I will thank you
to leave my orders to me.   I am perfectly aware
of the care you devote to your bi-weekly report,
short as, in all this business of invasion,
it too often has to be.   But these Christians
are my affair, and mine only.   They will die
when I decide—only I.   Is that clear ?


THE PREFECT

I have cause to suppose the infinite and hidden Majesty
grows slowly more inclined to think our health
cannot allow this sect.


THE MARSHAL

Do you tell me so ?
How kind, Prefect !   But I humbly laid, long since,
my poor thoughts on the matter before the Seclusion.


THE PREFECT

For a soldier, Excellency, you are curiously merciful.


THE MARSHAL

No, no.   I would not say so.   Economical,
you might call me perhaps ; more versed in tradition
than, by your permission, you founders of families
by your own genius and boldness can be.   I
come, you see, as a mere descendant of a house
for some generations permitted to serve P'o-l'u
in the more intimate dedications.   I have, it may be,
a certain hereditary intuition against your . . . daring.


THE PREFECT

The Sacred and Secluded Majesty—

### THE MARSHAL

There, you see !
How bold you are !  Now my—shall I say, tentacles ?—
quiver warnings to me at the touch of too much
bandying in commonplace talk of the Sacred Name.
Frame your own as you will, but, for your own sake,
I would not mistake what lies behind the mind of the Throne.
Absorb, absorb.

### THE PREFECT
Excellency, I did not mean—

### THE MARSHAL
I am sure, Prefect, you meant nothing indecorous.
Absorption, you know, is our central maxim of policy ;
absorption—no haste, no rashness ;
gentle, slow absorption.   Why do you think
I have gone to such quiet trouble to catch
this missionary, this wandering white priest ?
I would throw the Christians to the cephalopods now
if—In these seven-score isles we have seized,
there are Christians everywhere—yes ?

### THE PREFECT
Yes.

### THE MARSHAL

And then
beyond the mountains—when we get beyond the mountains—
there are more Christians—yes ?

### THE PREFECT
Yes.

### THE MARSHAL

And these,
if they become tiresome, we shall have to kill—
yes ?

THE PREFECT
Yes.


THE MARSHAL
Your eyes quite goggle.
I do not mesmerize you, I hope.   Pray
disagree, if you wish.   Do you wish to disagree ?


THE PREFECT
No.

THE MARSHAL
How wonderfully sympathetic you are !
Well then, we must kill if they are tiresome.
Now if we kill, they are wasted.   But they breed thickly,
these Christians ; and you know as well as I that of late
there has been remarked among us a spreading sterility—
as if we were much too intelligent or too powerful
for our own stock, as if we fed on ourselves,
and were everlastingly perishing.   It has been said
that, in places which neither you nor I will mention,
this has caused some anxiety.   Another fact
is that in the same unmentionable places destruction,
mere physical destruction—even by the suction
of cephalopods—is considered a poor substitution for the better
mental and spiritual absorption.   Your girl, now,
well—there she is.   But if by a small scare
or a small lure, she could have been brought to endure
—and then to enjoy—first the thought of the soldier,
and then the soldier, and then any soldier,
and then . . . men !   You see ?   And all the time
heartily thanking the merciful heart of P'o-l'u.
She, I allow, would have had no children.   But
there are others, and other ways for others.   You see ?
Agree, Prefect.

47

THE PREFECT
I agree.   But then, for that—

THE MARSHAL
For that we must creep deep into their mind,
and swallow them there.   The cephalopodic process
does not keep its lair only in the ocean.

THE PREFECT
And what has this to do with the missionary priest?

THE MARSHAL
He has been wandering here these many years,
founding churches, grounding their minds in belief.
He, I hope, is the channel by which now
I may come into them, and embrace them with mental
    tentacles,
and enlace them into P'o-l'u.

THE PREFECT
But how will you do that?

THE MARSHAL
Ah I cannot yet tell !   I cannot yet
at all guess where he may like to be tickled,
where his heart enjoys the thrilling titillation
of a mental indulgence.

THE PREFECT
But are you sure he will?

THE MARSHAL
No ; he may have just the necessary skill
to defeat me ; he may be one who rejects the sweet
psychic satisfaction.   I admit it.   But I have studied
all my life, my dear Prefect, the religious mind.

Every pious man—and, of course, woman—
has one—just one—surface where religion and he
are so delicately mixed in his soul as to be
indistinguishable ; he is never quite sure—
and does not (believe me !) ever want to be sure—
whether his religion or he is being soothed
into a lascivious spiritual delight.
All of them, Prefect, are at bottom religious lechers,
fornicating with their fancies.   These carved images
long before our time set up along the shore
are popular—like common brothels in the streets of P'o-l'u.
The Christian Church is a much grander affair,
kept with care—one of those rare buildings
(baths, scents, music, aphrodisiacs)
meant for the best of our families.   Well, we shall test
this fellow, swallow his children, repopulate P'o-l'u.
If *he* is caught, all the isles will follow.


                    THE PREFECT
It will take time.


                    THE MARSHAL
                    We have centuries.   And you,
you would warn the Sublime Throne—would you ?—
I am doing less than my duty !   Take care, Prefect !
Our Master's own cephalopods are very old
and very wise ; they are known to have taken a month
to squeeze a man slowly out of consciousness,
as he lies the while on the shore and is given food ;
unless the Infinite One, watching, took pity
and spoke under his infinite breath, and they finished
the wretch at once.   But that is most unlikely.


                    THE PREFECT
Excellency, I was only curious—

## THE MARSHAL

                              There is, besides,
behind the vast hall where he dwells by himself,
another hall, of green glass, filled
with giant ferns, and jade images of octopods,
where some, whom the Infinite Mercy after a week
bade the monsters release, wander mindless.
Or (which is worse) almost mindless, remembering,
when they see the jade shapes, their compressed muscles,
dodging among the ferns, hiding their eyes—
their food is dead fish dropped through a skylight,
their drink water from fountains, each fountain
surrounded by a lifelike tentacle.   In a gallery above
the ladies of the families make a habit of walking,
small, laughing lightly, talking scandal,
pointing at the mindless men in the hall.   Prefect,
this is the green-glassed centre of P'o-l'u.
True is it that the cephalopodic process
is not only physical.   Well . . . let us see.
Bid them bring in the traitor first ; and pray
stay here yourself.

                              [ASSANTU *is thrust in.*
                    Yes.   You were late.
We said the moon's fall ; it was sun's rise
before you reached my men.


## ASSANTU

                    Lord, we were late
starting ; besides, he went sadly and slowly.


## THE MARSHAL

Well.   What do you expect now ?


## ASSANTU

                              Freedom
to celebrate again the ancient initiation
and the favour of P'o-l'u for the adoration of the images.

Your people neglect them ?

ASSANTU
Since the Christians came.

THE MARSHAL
It may be we shall presently grant you leave.  First,
there is something else to do.  You are now mine,
and you will obey me.

ASSANTU
It was promised, lord—

THE MARSHAL
We and you have no common terms ;
therefore, no agreement.  P'o-l'u is unique.
If you need commonalty, you must believe other faiths—
the Christian and its Incarnation, for all I care.
Now you will obey us to whom you have given
yourself when you gave the priest.  You will go with him
back to the Christians—and whatever he may say
that you will follow and obey.

ASSANTU
But, lord—

THE MARSHAL
No, no, no buts ; you belong now to P'o-l'u,
since you served P'o-l'u : be still now and silent.
Our will is upon you, Assantu.  Have him in.
                              (*to* THE PREFECT)
                              [ANTHONY *is brought in*.
Bound ?  free him—and free that man.
I offer my apologies.  You will permit a few questions ?
You are the Christian priest in these Outer Seas ?

51

ANTHONY

Yes.

THE MARSHAL

You have been here at least twenty-five years ?
Fifteen in the northern parts ; but the last ten
passed mostly in this and the neighbouring isles.

ANTHONY

Yes ; that is roughly so.

THE MARSHAL

We know, of course,
about your success ; equally, we admire your devotion.
It must have been not without distress
you found yourself forced to abandon your folk.

ANTHONY

It was.

Very grave distress.

THE MARSHAL

Yes.   The reasons
that forced you to it no doubt seemed good,
as then understood.   I have the report somewhere.

ANTHONY

What knowledge or understanding can you possibly have
of me, or my reasons or actions ?

THE MARSHAL

Much every way.

We take care, before we approach the tiniest isle,
to be well aware of our . . . I do not wish to say ' foes ' . . .
No ; by your pardon, I will speak first.
You were caught in the act of . . . let us say, retreat ;
not running ; beyond the foothills it is difficult to run ;
but—

52

ANTHONY

That is an unworthy taunt.

THE MARSHAL

No taunt.

Think it a clumsy humour.   I cannot vaunt
my skill yet in this language.   Forgive me.   We heard
you loved your people.

ANTHONY

Dearly ; dearly.

THE MARSHAL

Yes.

And if you stayed, you expected martyrdom ?

ANTHONY

Martyrdom !

Should *I* have run from martyrdom ?

THE MARSHAL

See now !

It was not I who then said *run* . . .
Why are we standing ? let us sit down in comfort.
Prefect, a stool for our friend !   Squat, you.

(*to* ASSANTU).

Now, let us talk like gentlemen.   You had reasons.
Setting aside the natural fear of pain,
as unworthy you and me and this parley,
what, will you tell me, led you to leave your folk,
dearly loved, at such a dear moment ?
I do not ask idly ; I too have reasons.

ANTHONY

I need not give account of my reasons to any
but God and the Church.

53

THE MARSHAL

No, certainly.


ANTHONY

                I was forced

by much insistence to go.

      THE MARSHAL

             I will well believe it.


ANTHONY

There are things my people prize beyond life
and I beyond my seeming reputation.


THE MARSHAL

Truly : all religions have high secrets.
Why, I could tell you in our tradition—but pass.
You had your mission to preserve—


ANTHONY

     Not mine !


THE MARSHAL

                  Well,

you had your broader duty to do ;  and you believed
that your people here, you gone, would hold fast
to what they had received ?


ANTHONY

        I was—I *am* sure they will.


THE MARSHAL

You left them in fact almost for their own good ?

                  [ANTHONY *rises*.

No, please, father.   I understood—
no need for protestation.   It could be so.

Could be ?   Was.


THE MARSHAL
Was then : you did well.
You and I can speak not only as man to man,
and as soldier to soldier, but as general to general.   We
of the High Command do not leap in the first boat
or drop from the first plane.   We must school the rest
and rule them from a secluded, perhaps a hidden, head-
    quarters.
It cannot be otherwise.


ANTHONY
                    Make of it what you will.
Kill me if you choose ;  see if I fear death.


THE MARSHAL
Rid yourself of any such notion.
Our laws forbid ;  and the Nameless and Infinite Ruler.
We never persecute ;  indeed, we never execute
even our criminals.   In certain extreme cases—
treason, for example, or sacrilege—we do but leave
the sea, and the sea's inhabitants, free to act.
Is not that true, Prefect ?


THE PREFECT
                    Yes, Excellency.


THE MARSHAL
No ;  all this talk—you have been very kind—
had quite another purpose.   I wish to know
if you were a wise man or a foolish ;  if—
if you understood deeply how another's good
must always come before one's own ;  if
you could sacrifice yourself in a way perhaps more trying

than martyrdom ; if you could indeed give life,
and succeed.   Now I think of releasing you.

ANTHONY

Releasing !

THE MARSHAL

Restoring you to your place.   The unstable world needs
every pledge and grace of fidelity, all points
of ordination and relation.   The image of the Father—
to borrow a phrase of expression from your own speech—
must not be desecrated in any mode.

ANTHONY

The only image of the Father is the blessed Son.

THE MARSHAL

Say so, and yet the Son himself established
others in his own image—am I not right ?
Your people here are in a strange plight
and need you.   I would not have them false to you
lest the fidelity that straightens and stiffens the world
somewhat weaken.

ANTHONY

I am nothing ; the Faith all.

THE MARSHAL

You were to them the fatherhood in the Faith.
Losing your fatherhood—I do not say they would lose
the Faith ; but the terrible impersonality of faith
is hard for young souls.

ANTHONY

That is it ! that is it !

That is what I fear—that they should not be able to bear
in any crisis the dreadful abstract principles.

THE MARSHAL

You were right to fear.

ANTHONY

But then, sir, you—
why are you so tender for them ?

THE MARSHAL

I ?   Why, thus—
my master the Infinite Emperor is a father too,
and will be.   Into the sea of his extreme tenderness,
his avid care, must come the peoples Fate
gives him ; but then he is no rough lord.
He desires all to be in peace—believe
however they will, so they receive kindly
what kindly he gives.   I must a little fear
lest these childlike and rash pupils of yours,
for want of a word of advice, might ill judge,
and suffer then such ill as pure goodwill
would keep from them.   You and I would both fill
(might we so) their hearts with such conscience
as would earn much touch of blessing from the lord of P'o-l'u.

ANTHONY

But what is it then that you would have me do ?

THE MARSHAL

First, go back ; be to them again
all you were ; be father, pastor and master.
They cannot live unless you live by dying
a daily death for them.

ANTHONY

It is so, I know.

THE MARSHAL

We of the High Command must be spent so.

57

### ANTHONY

They grow from God's seed in our soil.

### THE MARSHAL

And our toil is always to supply their need. .

### ANTHONY

High as ever they reach, they spring from this.

### THE MARSHAL

And go much amiss if they disobey.

### ANTHONY

I would cherish and protect them.

### THE MARSHAL

So you may,
in—if I should say a small thing, you would be
on a sharp guard and look at once for deceit.
Well, I would not wake your doubt ; yet to spell
one word two ways is no great thing,
nor to separate two meanings in one sound,
if it were found proper.

### ANTHONY

Are you playing with me ?

### THE MARSHAL

No, by the heart of P'o-l'u !   It is one word
by which in our tongue we name the Emperor
and you in yours your God.   When you say God
we, as it happens, use the same syllable
for our master in the solemn rites.   Syllables to us
are traditional ; they have a civil value ; the hierarchy
is preserved honourably, generation after generation,
by this care.   It is no affair to be altered,

hastily, in a day, for a small, however sincere,
however—let us even allow—perhaps correct
sect—but small, I say, as to-day counts.


ANTHONY

This is hard.


THE MARSHAL
                    Not so hard, if the way be not barred
by a profane pseudo-religious obstinacy.
But this is clear—you, and you alone,
can discuss it in good sense with us of P'o-l'u.
You, and you alone, can explain all.
You are a father in the fatherhood ; do not disown
your duty to your children.


ANTHONY
I must think of this.


THE MARSHAL
                                        Do so.
But first, for all our sakes, be again
their teacher and elder.   In all pieties a preacher
or a priest rules—except in such lewd
and crude unwrapping of marvels as this fellow,
retching here, yellow with fear, might devise,
were he not under your eyes.   But no priest
nor preacher can rightly initiate conduct unless
the Fatherhood profess in him its original mystery.


ANTHONY
The Fatherhood chooses as it will for that.


THE MARSHAL
                                        True,
and has chosen.   It was you whom here first it chose,

and though when these troubles began you might well suppose
you should lie hidden, yet now, being bidden out,
to take again your fatherhood were wisely done.
It was you by whom their new life was begun ;
let it continue in you.

ANTHONY

I promise nothing.


THE MARSHAL

When I ask your promise, refuse it if you choose.
Your people are in your church.   I had search made
for them particularly along all the shore.
Now I restore them to you and you to them—
one lacking, alas !   She was rash, and my men ;
and in a flash of temper. . . Had you been here—
you were not.

ANTHONY

What has happened ?


THE MARSHAL

Had you been here—
Do not leave these childish folk again.
Let it be ;—no ; you will hear.   My dear Prefect,
will you tell our guards the Christians within are free
to come and talk here—not to wander.
The sentries yonder have been given orders to shoot.

[THE PREFECT *goes into the church and in a moment
returns with the* SOLDIERS.

Here is your guide and fellow-prisoner ; he
is free too, to go with you as you will.

[ASSANTU *rises*.   ANTHONY *speaks to him*.   THE
MARSHAL *meets* THE PREFECT.

I think I may claim the cephalopodic process
is beginning with some success.   Gentleness and sweetness
are more entangling tentacles, Prefect, than rifles.

THE PREFECT

It needs your skill, Excellency.

THE MARSHAL

You are too kind.
I will see you again presently (*to* ANTHONY).

[THE MARSHAL *and* THE PREFECT *go out.*

ASSANTU

Will you come to the church ?

ANTHONY

Wait a moment ;  I must have a moment's prayer
before I meet my children.

[THE FLAME *comes from the church.*

THE FLAME

Prayer ?   I am there.

ANTHONY

Blessed Spirit, show me what I should do.

THE FLAME

Indeed . . . but most prayer is instruction to him.

ANTHONY

Since I have been brought back to these again,
it is clear I am more needed here than elsewhere.

THE FLAME

If indeed you can be said to be needed at all.

ANTHONY

Else, our retirement must have succeeded better.
I have more good to do them, more help
to bring—

61

### THE FLAME

O son, do the saints pray thus?
Do you forget you were bought at a great price?
It is your friends who pay part of the price
in learning from you ; this is their happy sacrifice,
and your profit on someone else's purchase.

### ANTHONY

I wish only to give myself for their good—

### THE FLAME

—and your goods to the poor and your body to be burned,
    and if
the will of charity is not there still,
what good then will be the good you do?
Do you not know that not until you have sold
all that is in you for the poor, can you follow Christ?
All—including the knowledge that you give it to the poor.

### ANTHONY

Give me therefore grace—

### THE FLAME

This is the grace—
this distraction that disturbs your prayer, lest the prayer
prove to you—poor child !—an unfair burden.

### ANTHONY

—to be to them a tender father and wise ;
grant that on the foundation they find in me
they may build a true church, low but well-roofed.
Grant this, blessed Spirit, and bless
me to my task, whatever their present want.

### THE FLAME

So let it be. But their want perhaps is more
than you could guess before, or can now.

## ANTHONY

As for this trouble of a word, with me to show,
it may go well enough.   The spirit matters
more than the letter.  It were better to let slide
some jot or tittle, that has in its mere self
little significance than to split peace wide.
It is fit, if possible, not to antagonize souls
by the more-or-less, the give-and-take, of words :
better that quarrels should cease, and peace live.


## THE FLAME

It is, we of heaven agree, a thing indifferent ;
but any indifference may become sometimes a test.
Will God dispute over words ? no ; but man
must, if words mean anything, stand by words,
since stand he must ; and on earth protest to death
against what at the same time is a jest in heaven.
Alas, you are not in heaven ! the jests there
are tragedies on earth, since you lost your first poise
and crashed.  Yet pray that his will be done on earth
as it is in heaven—tragedy or jest or both,
and so let it be.  Do you know, Anthony, what I say ?


## ANTHONY

If they obey, I will strike the rock and cry :
' Water, flow ! '  So I have done, and so
will do now.   Out of my poise of judgment
they shall leap certainly to their everlasting joys.
Amen.

*[He remains silent.*


## THE FLAME

Amen.   What do you say, Assantu ?


## ASSANTU

I will bring all my people back to me.

63

### THE FLAME

That is honest, at least.

### ASSANTU

     We will feast by the fires
that shall flicker below the faces of the carved images
on the flesh of boars and bulls named and slain.

### THE FLAME

Without shedding of blood is no remission of sins.
This, except in P'o-l'u, is understood everywhere ;
P'o-l'u only has no sins to remit.
But be free, Assantu, be free ; see what you can.
Come from the circumference, both of you, into the centre.
       *[He touches* ASSANTU's *head.*

### ASSANTU

O now the fire that walks in the jungle
astonishes my brain with promise. O Tantula,
Tantula, you shall be but one of a number ; again
we will offer other sacrifice than boars and bulls.

### THE FLAME

The blood of Tantula cries to me from the ground.
Look in it, Assantu !

### ASSANTU

      Sacrifice of men !
Others to be our offering, and their skulls made
more than boars or bulls our safe preservative.
We shall live and they die—

### THE FLAME

      So all !
Ask your hearts, my people, ask your hearts.
         *(to the audience).*
There are few of you here who do not prefer to walk

with the old man on the new way, and talk
with the ghouls and goblins of your own souls rather
than with us of heaven who were given to you for companions :
Count all—Anthony, Assantu, P'o-l'u, and you.
. . . Enough.

[*He goes into the church.*

ANTHONY
Go, Assantu ; call my friends.


ASSANTU (*near the church*)
Siru ! Siru !

SIRU (*coming out*)
That was a voice I knew.
It cannot be—

ASSANTU
Yes, Siru, it is I.


SIRU
Why, Assantu ! . . . What has happened ?


ASSANTU
As things do.
Our start too late, their disembarkation too soon,
the moon sunk and an ambush set in the hills
which we met.

SIRU
You were taken prisoner ?


ASSANTU
And brought back
down the track we had followed three hours before.


SIRU
But our father ?

ASSANTU

O your father is here safely ;
you need not fear for him.

ANTHONY

Here, Siru !

[SIRU *runs to him.*

SIRU

Father !
[*He kneels for* ANTHONY's *blessing.*
But tell me what happened.   Are you come
to join us in death ? is there to be no breath
in God's Church here but that of the Spirit himself
till a new mission be sent ?

ANTHONY

Do not despair.
A new way may perhaps be begun
where we least expect, and an all but spent fire
flare suddenly into heat.   As for what happened—
it is easy to tell.   Assantu led me safely
up through the first foothills towards the pass—
but I slow to go for age and heaviness.
When the moon sank we had come to the last strange
carved image, set on a platform of its own
where vegetation ceases and rocks begin.
There we rested ; in the first thin light
pressing upward we went past that shape,
which, of all of them, looks most like a man,
an old petrified man staring at the sea,
and thinking our escape sure, stumbling on—

SIRU

But to delay there !   Why, Assantu
could go as far at night as any by day.

No ; not with a foreigner and an old man.

ANTHONY

Danger to go, danger to stay.  We stayed—
partly perhaps to let my breath come.
O wisely, it now seems, I had hesitated here ;
I should have waited, as something in me bade.
Suddenly they leapt on us out of the rocks ;
death in their rifles and in their faces, death
in their hands on us, and their cries ; well, there
they bound us, and so, under God's will, we returned—
to live or die, my sons in Christ, with you.
You may guess if my heart burned in me by the way.
It is well to be in time ; perhaps, by that grace,
our Lord will have us live and not die.

SIRU

This is strange and difficult !  That they should lie there,
not so difficult ; they are subtle to do harm.
But that Assantu should take no alarm—
the very smell of their nearness in the morning air
would have reached me, and I nothing to compare with him
in swiftness of sense.

ASSANTU

You must take it the Father made dense
the skill of my flesh for the better fetching of his will
for your designs.

ANTHONY

Yes ! and these things signs
we shall sail perhaps on a course we did not think,
to a new land, and not sink in the storm.

SIRU

I do not understand ; what new land ?
One of us is already dead : what land ?

ANTHONY

One of the Church ?

SIRU

Alayu, the daughter of Oloya ;
not an hour since, under P'o-l'u's rifles.

ANTHONY

But—

SIRU

Come and pray beside her.

ANTHONY

I will,
immediately ; the Lord receive her soul.

[*A moment's silence.*
But—

why she ?   It was not for her faith ? no ;
he swore they did not persecute.

ASSANTU

I knew Alayu.
She had no faith ; she wanted tender promises
till she was married.   She was as soft as a plum
with as hard a heart.

ANTHONY

Where did she die ?

SIRU

There :
where you are standing.

ANTHONY

But why and how—tell me.
Peace be with her.

68

SIRU

And on all of us the Peace.
One of their officers questioned us ; catching at him,
she was struck down by his men.

ANTHONY

An accident then ?

ASSANTU

I am sure in her fear she swore she did not believe.

ANTHONY

No ; she would not, or—did she ?
This was what I had much in mind !
I warned you, Siru.

ASSANTU

I know I am right ; did she ?
Answer us, Siru.

SIRU

She did ; she denied all.

ANTHONY

Alas, poor child !   The fear of this fretted me.

SIRU

So that now we do not know what ' to live ' means
in your sense ; we must have another ' to live '.

ASSANTU

No ; I think you will not last long.

SIRU

Will you too wrong us ? will you be apostate too ?

ASSANTU

Wait a little, and we shall all see.

## SIRU

And see everything, and see with clear eyes.
You cannot surprise our Lord with the terror of death.

## ASSANTU

No ?   There are others it seems possible to terrify.

## ANTHONY

Hush, Assantu ; this is wild talk.
So young a child, and if I had been here,
I might have set all right.

## SIRU

                      Our Lord, sir,
will do that.   It may be that her last scream
was no more than a cry in child-birth, when he was born
piercingly in her soul, and her very death
her first motherly waking.

## ANTHONY

                      Hush, Siru.
Apostasy is always apostasy.

## SIRU

                    I am sorry, father.

## ANTHONY

Assantu and you are fallen to the two extremes
of anger and apology.   It seems it is time I took
the shepherd's crook again.   Go, call
all the Church here : tell them I am here.
I will pray presently by this unhappy girl
who should—could she—have been a witness to Christ.

## SIRU

She died, even if she lied ; she is still a witness.

Might not, sir, her first baptismal vow
have swallowed her fault, instead of her fault her vow ?
If God is outside time, is it so certain
that we know which moments of time count with him,
and how ?

ANTHONY

Enough ; no more argument now.
Call the Church.   I will not speak by her body
lest it raise quarrels—as here between you two.
[SIRU *goes into the church.*
You, Assantu, are a zealot ; that is good,
but we must not make your nature into a rule
for all ; you are blest in it ; but for the rest—
be tender, son.   Siru is a good man.

ASSANTU (*looking after* SIRU)
My zeal shall go further than Siru has gone,
and make his head into one of those. . . . You said ?

ANTHONY
We must have quiet souls.   Now I am back
they shall not lack counsel or command.   O if—
if we might bring the Cross even to P'o-l'u !
No missionary has ever reached there—
ships cast away or turned from the port—
but O if now I, by a fair chance,
might . . . a little tact, a little care !

ASSANTU
Do you think to convert P'o-l'u ?

ANTHONY

I hardly dare,
yet—It is true I have been for twenty-five years
a wanderer in these lands.   O if now these hands

might pour the water of heaven on the sons of P'o-l'u,
that would be indeed a climax. Who knows?

ASSANTU

Weariness has made you mad.

ANTHONY

                                    Blessed madness !
The Universal Church would well be eased
with this last miasma of mystical paganry
dispersed, and the last shire of the world held
by me for Christ ! It cannot be, and yet he,
not we, chooses apostles and gives sons.

ASSANTU

It is clear, father, you take yourself to be someone.

ANTHONY

Who was it said the Fatherhood must have its way?

ASSANTU

To eat ; but Siru or you will serve for me.

ANTHONY

Anything I can do to serve you, son, I will do.

ASSANTU

I think so ; but which of us knows best how?

                    [SIRU *returns with* THE CHORUS.

SIRU

I have told them what I know. Say your will.

ANTHONY

God's blessing on you, children.

72

### THE CHORUS
And on you, father.

### ANTHONY

I had rather a thousand times be restored thus
than safe across the mountains.   Little children,
see how God rules all to good,
and that more than any of us understood.
Now we shall live or die together.   Whether
death is as near as lately we were bound to fear
we shall see.

### SIRU
We have seen.   We saw Alayu die.


### ANTHONY

Yes ; well . . . that was tragic.   Yet—
believe me, Siru, I do not think less
than how her death must grieve us all ;  the more,
in the manner it was.   Yet—let us speak it out—
her death strips a weak branch from the Church.
It is the price of our wholeness.   All is ruled
so that even our pain at such denial is our gain.
So it has been since Christ first built
the new man on his own plan of bones—
sacrifice after sacrifice.   We must not make
a girl's sin or a soldier's folly or fury
the measure of the future ;  a future, I dare to say,
which has more to pay in joy than ever we supposed.


### SIRU

Father Anthony, we saw Alayu die.
It were idle to think that these men will not kill
whenever they choose.

### ANTHONY
Peace, Siru, peace.
I perhaps have been saved for this and sent

to be to you no abstract direction from afar
but a more visible father.   I have come again
to be your father, you, my first-fruits of salvation.
I have a thought now that our new vocation
may spread over all the isles.

OROYO
                          On my own island
I have heard of what these creatures do to Christians.
Do not be deceived ; they are devils all.

ANTHONY
Hush, son.   Christ is their brother and ours.

TORNA
Indeed so ; but we, you said, must be
his witnesses—even if they kill us.

ANTHONY
                                If they will.
If they will not—
                  SIRU
                          Father, you have come again
to be our fellow and friend.   So, good.
But there is a knowledge in us we cannot share.
We have seen blood ; we have seen the end of this world.

ANTHONY
Do you think I, who am twice as old as you,
have not seen death ?   I, when I was young,
saw my mother die, and lacked her a thousand years.
A child's tears are never wholly stayed
through the man's life afterwards ; his heart feels
a full trench, and nothing heals the grief.
Come ; this is foolish talk ; we must think
the living need us.

OROYO

That is true.


TORNA

Say your meaning.


ANTHONY

This.   If God show us a field to reap,
I would have you ready, children, to yield to his will.
I have talked with the leader of P'o-l'u ; he wishes truce
between themselves and us.   I have thought of it
and think we should do well to take his word
rather than defy him and die.


SIRU

We shall not defy.
God, who only lives, cannot defy,
and cannot die ; nor cannot live with a life
other than his own.


ANTHONY

It is hardly fit, son,
you alone should set yourself against me.
I am older than you ; I have studied the Faith more,
and wear the priesthood.


SIRU

What does this truce mean ?


ANTHONY

I am not to be questioned overmuch.
I will decide, and guide you.   This leader of P'o-l'u
himself believes in some sort of omnipotent Father,
by whom in a short time we may show him ours.
You, Assantu, you heard him ; is it not so ?

ASSANTU

It is.


SIRU

      Sir, you have not to call witnesses.
P'o-l'u has its father, I concede ; we saw
and heard something of him.   Another captain
gave us details of where his servants lurk,
and the work they do.   That is his truce ; good.
We will give him no excuse to make another.


ANTHONY

That is flat insolence, Siru.


SIRU

                        No.

Only Alayu's body lies between us
and the end of this world ; and her true voice,
the voice of Alayu the Christian, takes my breath
perhaps from beyond death.


ASSANTU

                You are a fool.
No woman lives beyond . . . but have your way.
The ocean, and certain things in it, will cool
this passion of yours.


ANTHONY

         Hush, Assantu !   Children,
I have come back to you out of death—


SIRU

No, father, only from this side death.
We saw Alayu *die*.

76

OROYO
        And that is true.
Siru, I do not understand all you say,
but this day made a sudden breach in my heart,
and half of it is yours.

ANTHONY
        It is I who do not understand.
I came, if you must quibble, from this side death,
looking for the joy of your old obedience ; thence
peace and the fruits of the Spirit.

THE FLAME (*coming out*)
        Who named us ?

TORNA
Let the Spirit judge between us.

THE FLAME
        So we will.

Hither, spirits ! come you all together.
        (*to* THE CHORUS).

Take our will, the final skill to speak,
the final compulsion upon you to speak truly,
as if at very judgment.   Now, Anthony,
what do you wish ?

ANTHONY (*slowly*)
        I would . . . I would be again
all that which I was to these once,
their father, their centre, almost their creator.

THE FLAME (*to* THE CHORUS)
        Reply.

77

### The Chorus

Wisely we did to send and you to go,
and piety always we have for the past ; but now
we too are older ; nothing can be as it was.
A friend is come out of the Fatherhood ; the Fatherhood
lives only in the sweet duty to the friend.

### Anthony

I wish you to spring from me and live from me.

### The Chorus

The new life must be ours and not yours ;
God is our cause of being, and only God.

> [Anthony *tries to speak and fails.*

### The Flame

We lay our common will upon you ; speak.
Say the truth, and hear what you say.

### Anthony (*as if under compulsion*)

I do not wish you to live from God alone ;
I wish always to be your means of God.

### The Chorus

That, if it could be, we too
would willingly enjoy.   It is not we who long
to mature, and endure the pure autonomy of souls,
but only so shall we ever be true sons.

### Anthony

Am I no more than you ?

### The Chorus

Nor we than you.
Each of us all is a single conjunction with God
to function so.

ANTHONY (*struggling*)
No . . . no . . . no ;
I will not say . . . I do not mean . . . this.


THE FLAME
Say.


ANTHONY
It is not true.


THE FLAME
Say.


ANTHONY
No ;
I could not mean . . . I could not . . .


THE FLAME
The art of heaven
knows your heart ; heaven is always exact ;
and shall give you an interpreter, whose mouth is more frank
to say wholly what you mean. Assantu, speak.


ASSANTU
I wish not to be eaten, but to eat others ;
I wish to grow great and thrive on others ;
and if others will not, I wish them to be compelled.
I will be a belly to them and they food to my belly.


THE FLAME
Our Father retracts himself in his own nature—
for his Son in himself and on earth for every creature ;
this is the good of fatherhood—to be food,
and an equal friend in the end, and blessèd if so.

79

ANTHONY

No ! but to lose the past—

THE FLAME

            The past is now ;
you will only enjoy either by being both—
else your sloth will be a creeping octopus.
Go on ; say what you wish more.

ANTHONY

I wish them to be content to use the Name
for the centre of P'o-l'u ; no blame in it
if we explain it away, and a chance that I
shall be called by and by the apostle of P'o-l'u.

THE CHORUS

Do you direct this as a priest of Christ ?

ANTHONY

I claim at least the prestige of the priesthood.

THE CHORUS

There is no prestige in any blessed priesthood,
only the priesthood ; no prestige in any
true thing, but God and the thing itself.
We saw Alayu die.

ANTHONY

            Why say so now ?

THE CHORUS

Death, friend, teaches us many things.
Ours is a world without opinions ; here
everything is what it is, and nothing else.
And now, whatever may be at other times,
we will not use the same language as P'o-l'u,
who slew Alayu.

ANTHONY

       After she betrayed the Faith,
and was by her own act excommunicate.


SIRU

You of other lands may separate so ;
we cannot.   We in these isles
live in our people—no man's life his own—
from birth and initiation.   When our salvation
came to us, it showed us no new mode—
sir, dare you say so ?—of living to ourselves.
The Church is not many but the life of many
in ways of relation.   This new birth
was common to Alayu and to us ; no sin,
no death through sin, no death in sin,
parts us.   It is sin, you say, our Lord redeems
in his Church ; how if he now redeem this ?


ANTHONY

If indeed she had repented before she died—


SIRU

Sir, we lay there our hands on our mouths.
See, because of her death we live more strong
in his clear goodness—much less doubt,
less fear ; this is God's way—
to cause his day to dawn in sheer blood.
It is she, let me say, as well as you, to whom
we owe now all that we know of grace.


ANTHONY

This is unbelievable and unbearable.
Do you say that this apostate woman and I
are equally profitable to you ?

SIRU

Sir, why not ?
Thus it becomes us to be her friends and yours,
her children even ; she died without children,
but her blood has mothered us in the Faith, as yours fathered.


ANTHONY

This is sheer and absolute lunacy and heresy—


THE FLAME

Assantu will say it better ; speak, Assantu.


ASSANTU

You who have gone astray from the Father and me,
you who will not be eaten of your betters, you
who have wandered away from the images, and thrown by
all that of old was true—there is a way
waiting for you in the dead waters, and beyond
is the land of rotting flesh and chirruping souls
and the everlasting eating.  A fire consumes me ;
I must have you for my own, wholly my own, none
shall have you but I.  I am the Father, and hungry—


ANTHONY

Jesu God Almighty have mercy upon me !
I do not—I will not—know what I am saying.


THE FLAME

You were praying to my lord the Spirit for exactly that.


ANTHONY

I never wanted that—


THE FLAME

O but you did.
Rid yourself, my son, of all deceit.

82

ANTHONY

But I may be right—


THE FLAME

                    Yes ; you may be right,
but to be right in the devil is to be wrong in the Spirit,
and yet, even in the devil, right is right.
Blessed and praised and glorious for ever be he
who will have us right all ways, not only one.
Glory, everlasting glory, for this grace—


THE CHORUS

—be to the Father and the Son and the Holy Spirit !
        [THE MARSHAL *and* THE PREFECT *come in abruptly.*
            THE FLAME *hides himself.*


THE MARSHAL

All together ?   I hope, agreed ?   No doubt
some little hesitation ? you will find it work out,
if you give it time.   Can you say anything ?

                                (*to* ANTHONY).


ANTHONY

                                        I ? . . .
What have I to say ?   What . . . I do not understand :
what decision do you need so fast ?


THE MARSHAL

                                Come,
you said you have reasons ; so have I now.
The answer ?


ANTHONY

            But what ? to what ? I am a poor
sinful man—

                        83

Never mind sin now.
Will you take my former offer or die ?   I see
you have no conclusion to report.   Time is short,
but you shall have till morning.   Before moonset I shall come.
I advise you to manage to agree to some compromise.
Your god is young and can afford to change his name ;
ours is old.

SIRU
That—

ANTHONY
A moment, friend.
This, between brothers, is my office.
He has ended deception and mended what was amiss.
Our God, sir, has all time to his Name,
being the Ancient of Days and the Youngest Day.
There is no god but he.

THE MARSHAL
We shall see that.

ANTHONY
I find that at last there is nothing else to see.
Come, brothers, let us before night
say the Rite together.
                    [*He goes to the church.*   THE CHORUS *follow.*

THE MARSHAL (*to* ASSANTU)
Wait, you.
                    [*He beckons and a* SOLDIER *comes in with* RAIS.
We found late this woman straggling.   Your wife ?

ASSANTU
She may say so ; but a lord of the sacrifice has no wife.

THE MARSHAL (*to* THE PREFECT)

Everywhere the same language ! the Christians and he
babble one talk.   One might think their speech
was flung, like falling fire, about the world
which all watch and catch, and syllable in frenzy,
each a match for the other.   But we know
where all the mad significance of speech ends
in the emptiness of the hall of the infinite and sublime
Nameless
among his cephalopods : space and nothing . . . I am
dizzy . . .
Well, take her !                                    (*to* ASSANTU).
                  I bring her to help snare
the white priest mentally as you did physically.
Better lose no time.


ASSANTU
Sir, now
I think of other things.


THE MARSHAL
The worse for you.

Go !

[ASSANTU *and* RAIS *withdraw*.


THE PREFECT
Excellency, why so much haste ?


THE MARSHAL

Indeed, I had spaced it better ; but to-night
I hear messages and instructions through the air.
The sea-borne Powers, the dying creatures of dream,
have gathered a kind of fleet.   It is thought well
to swell our farther armies with ships and men.
We must not cross the mountains.   I leave here

85

seven companies—and you, Prefect, at their head.
I and the rest set out to-morrow for P'o-l'u.

THE PREFECT

But surely we destroyed them by sea and air.

THE MARSHAL

Not enough.

The Admiral muddled the affair ; he is a fool.
One of these new unfamilied men.   Of course,
in the end . . . but I must not now spare the time
to prepare and school the Christians in their comic parts,
and watch their hearts sucked into P'o-l'u.

THE PREFECT

But I—

THE MARSHAL

Come.   No ; you are a strong man,
Prefect, but a little drastic for comedy.   Farce,
perhaps.   Come, you must write your report to-night.
You would not—would you ?—forget your last opportunity ?
I will do myself the pleasure of carrying it in person to P'o-l'u.

[They go out.

## ACT III

*It is moonlight again.* THE CHORUS *are asleep about the stage,
except* ASSANTU, *who is brooding near the trees with* RAIS
*watching him, and* ANTHONY *who is praying at the back
near the church.* THE FLAME *comes from the church.*

### THE FLAME

This night is mine, and for mine.   Dreams
are naught, except I put a thought in them.
Deeper and deeper let the pure night fall
in which, till the sun come, we are the light ;
this is the night when souls become themselves,
and dreams become thoughts and thoughts acts.
Sleep ; but awake, you spirits, in the world of spirit ;
be aware of the great affair of conclusion.   Earth
concludes, and feuds (except in P'o-l'u) end.

*[He moves among the sleepers.*

Where there is yet sin left, where
you are not yet bereft of indirection,
see now that to which you cling.
Oroyo, you are apt to be impatient ; do you feel
the angers ? the moving rocks clapt together
and you barely safe ?   You were used to be shy,
Torna, among your friends, but I now
will have you rarely fine as a guide to others,
your brothers of to-morrow.   And you, Siru, you have died
to sin, and soon I will set you free from sorrow.
And you, the messenger of our tongue, my son Anthony ?

87

ANTHONY

Lord, let it plague me still to feel my folly.


THE FLAME

What in you was public is private in all ;
it is a common dream ; but whom we mean
to spare hereafter, we commonly endanger now.


ANTHONY

I was a stranger and foreigner in the Faith I professed.


THE FLAME

No ; only you were willing to rest in supposing
the Faith was for you and not you for the Faith.
Out of which dreams come, themes
of sad nightmare.   Let us see now of what kind
such dreams, yours and all men's, are :
ask your hearts, my people, ask your hearts !

> [*He hides himself, and withdraws to the church.*

This is the universal deceit ; let us see
how it shows visibly.   We—my companions and I—
withdraw ; and do you, moon, fail from the skies !
Natural light dies with the supernatural.
Rise, fantasies ! lies of the soul, rise !


ASSANTU (*muttering*)

Sacrifice : sacrifice : the sacrifice of a man !
That in the hour of death gives power
more than bulls to come past the All-Hungry
and be myself an eater in the empty isles.
O to consume and not to be consumed !

> [*The moonlight begins to alter to a glow of decay.*
> ANTHONY *rises stiffly and turns.*   THE CHORUS
> *raise themselves stiffly towards him.   The voices*
> *become inhuman.*

ANTHONY

Everyone adores me and I no one—


THE CHORUS

Everyone adores you and you no one—


ANTHONY

Except, of course, God.


THE CHORUS

Except, of course . . .

[*They get stiffly to their knees, stretching their arms out towards him.*


ANTHONY

I am for each of you the only father—


THE CHORUS

You are for each of us the only father—


ANTHONY

Except, of course, God.


THE CHORUS

Except . . .

[ANTHONY *moves slowly towards them ; their hands touch him.*


ANTHONY

Love me . . . love me . . . love me.


THE CHORUS

We love you . . . we love you . . . we love you.


ANTHONY

Except, of course, God.

### THE CHORUS

Except . . .

*[THE CHORUS are silent. Their hands clasp him.*
*The light has wholly changed.*

### THE CHORUS

Come down to us ; come down to us.

### ANTHONY

So I will ; so I do ; warm—
it is warm here.

### THE CHORUS (*dispersedly*)

It is warm ; come down.
Father, father, father, father, father !

### ANTHONY

It is dark here : only your eyes are bright,—
but they do not see me ! there is no meaning in your eyes.
Your hands are hard.

### THE CHORUS

The better to hold you with,
the better to draw you down.

### ANTHONY

What do you say ?

### THE CHORUS

We say only what you told us to say :
Father, father, father, father, father !
here where we are meaningless, you are meaningless.

*[The arms are wrapped round him.*

Press ; squeeze.

ANTHONY
Not so tight.

THE CHORUS
                              Press ; squeeze.
Tighter ; tighter.

ANTHONY
You are strangling me.

THE CHORUS
                              Dear father !
we love you ; we adore you ; you wanted us to love you.
How we love you ! we only live in this love.
You loved love and love is what you shall have.
                              [*The light goes out.*
Father, father !

ANTHONY (*choking*)
Help !

THE CHORUS
                              Thus we adore.
                    [THE FLAME *is seen in a fiery light.*

THE FLAME
More perhaps, even in a dream, would madden you—
to see the spiritual octopus clutching a man's soul.
Anthony, can you hear me ?

ANTHONY
                    Yes . . . yes . . . O voice,
voice of something that was, draw me up.

THE FLAME
While you can hear me, you are not wholly damned,
even in a dream.   Do you remember Alayu ?

ANTHONY

Alayu ?

THE FLAME

She who died excommunicate.

ANTHONY

Yes.

THE FLAME

Fall, fantasies ! lies in the soul, fall !
Rise, again, moon ! and, light, return.
Alayu !

> [*The ghost of* ALAYU *enters from the church. The
> moonlight returns.* ANTHONY *is standing in the
> centre, but* THE CHORUS *are asleep as at the
> beginning.*

THE FLAME

I stand between the living and the dead.
See each the other ; see and speak.

RAIS

Why do you stare so ?

ASSANTU

I cannot see
the shapes I hear.   I hear voices near
of the jungle and the ocean and the full moon : hush !

ANTHONY

Alayu !

ALAYU

Sir, I am sorry I was afraid.
Will you forgive me and will the Church forgive ?
I am sent to ask this.

ANTHONY
                Sin is deeper—
and I caught in it—than ever I thought.
How can I have any right to forgive ?
Ask our Lord ; he is the only-adored ;
he alone forgives.

                ALAYU
                So I do,
but a tongue of flame sent me to ask you.

                ANTHONY
Can I, spent in sin, can I forgive ?
I am worse than you.

                THE FLAME
                That is certainly true,
but how can you be forgiven if you yourself,
for whatever virtuous reason, do not forgive ?
It is your function ; be ashamed, but try.

                ALAYU
Will you ?

                ANTHONY
                Wholly ; I solely am to blame,
and the shame is mine.

                ALAYU
                No.   Just as I died,
I knew it was true, all the same.

                ANTHONY
                                                What ?

                ALAYU
What you said ; what I believed ; love.
                        93

ANTHONY (*shuddering*)

Love !

ALAYU

Love was so much better than you said.
I had been thinking of it and waiting for it,
expecting and selecting it, drinking the dream in
at the blessed feast, losing the feast in the dream,
confusing it with you and Siru : O stupid !
and then suddenly I was knocked into commonsense ;
I knew, whatever it was, it was not so.
I may learn yet. What I owe to P'o-l'u !
Tell me, friend and father, what can I do
to show I am sorry I was such a sensual slut
while I thought I was only being Christian.

ANTHONY

But—

I see and speak to you, yet I know you are spirit.
You are one of the dead.

ALAYU

Yes truly ; but you said
we were dead in Christ ; there is nothing new in being dead.
I know that now. But what shall I do ?

ANTHONY

Blessed daughter, can I give orders to the dead ?

THE FLAME

No, but I will ; or at least propose parity.
I stand between the charity of the living and the dead.
Alayu, you who could not bear death
through falseness of love, if this man were to die,
could you bear his natural fear ?

ALAYU

Be afraid again ?

O !

THE FLAME

Or continue a slut in death.

ALAYU

O ! . . .

I suppose so, by God's help, if I must.
Must I ?

THE FLAME

Or be a silly tippler in love.

ANTHONY

That was I—a drunkard in adoration.
O salvation is rare, bare, and steep.
What are you, spirit ?

THE FLAME

One of the masters of exchange.
Let it rest at that.   You talked much, Anthony,
in a grand rhetorical Christianity, of what you owed
your fellows and children in the Faith.   Now will you owe,
in no vanity of the general but in one particular,
a debt to this—what did you call her ?—apostate ?

ANTHONY

I thought I spoke the truth.

THE FLAME

I know you did.
But then the Faith is much truer than you thought.

95

If—as you may yet—you come to the octopus,
will you be content that this girl shall bear
your fear? for (make no mistake) you will be afraid,
deadly afraid.  You prayed for strength ; here
is the answer God sends.  Will you take the answer?


ANTHONY

I am to owe her my own salvation from apostasy?


THE FLAME

It may be.  Will you?


ANTHONY

           If she and God will.


THE FLAME

Blessed is the intercession of all souls.
Alayu, you are dead ; you have nothing yourself to fear
but something to do, and if that should be to fear,
it is still something to do.  In a dream you desired
the Faith : will you redeem faith and desire
by saving another to be nothing but glad in death?


ALAYU

Yes.  It will not—will it?—last long.


THE FLAME

As soon as you know it indeed, it will be past.


ALAYU

I keep on being a fool.  I meant—yes.


THE FLAME

Blessed they who confess the Christ so.
You shall find the blessing.  This is the mind of the Church—

to discover always the way of the lover and the love.
The young shall save the old and the old the young,
the dead the living, and the other living the dead,
and my tongue shall tell in heaven the truth of all.
Return again, till I call you, to the cloud of ascension,
Alayu ; and you, Anthony, to peace in prayer.

> [ANTHONY *kneels*. THE FLAME *and* ALAYU *go to*
> *the door of the church.*


ASSANTU

I begin to see the shapes : something moves.
There, over there, the fire's edge in the jungle !


RAIS

Where ?


ASSANTU

      There ; it is burning through my brain.
cutting it in two.   One side is dying ;
the other is trying to know what to do.
My head ! my head !


RAIS

               Husband, turn to me !


ASSANTU

I cannot run ; I have not stopped running
since last night they drew the snare tight.
When they turned us there, my turnings ended,
and ever since I have done nothing but run
straighter and straighter ; whatever I seemed to be doing
I was running down the lonely track of the dead
where is no way back, but P'o-l'u behind.
Presently I shall run as fast as the fire.

No.

Turn to me ; I am your wife ; here
in my arms !   I will hold you so that you cannot run.

[*She tries to embrace him.*

Assantu

You ? no ; you are holding someone ; whom
are you holding ? whose face looks—Tantula !
it is Tantula ; that is right ; hold him fast.
I told, you to hold him : there is no room for me.
Besides, you have no life but in your flesh.
There is no canoe for you to the dolorous shore ;
you shall drift, as women do, along the waters.
P'o-l'u and I do not want you.

Rais

P'o-l'u,

now, has no use even for you.
It will kill you soon.

Assantu

Hold Tantula ! O
my brain is nearly cut through.   But
the old man was slow—so slow !
it is he who keeps me back now, I know.

The Flame

Come quickly, come quickly, Assantu.
In the jungle my companions and I do nothing but run,
all the forces of nature loosed on a creature.
Only in the church we run and are still at once ;
so it is willed where will and power are one.
Outside, everything, without guide, runs.
Run fast, Assantu, run fast.

## ASSANTU

Yes, but I must rid myself of the old man.
He is tied to my side. Since we were caught by P'o-l'u
he has always hindered me. Rais cannot help ;
her embrace is round Tantula ; her face on his.
If now the old man were dead
he could run quickly before me to the shore of grief.
O ! O !

## RAIS

Husband !

## ASSANTU

Hush ! . . . It is done.
My brain is burned right through. Why,
where is Tantula ? have you let him go ?
he was not quite dead, was he ? O
but now everything is easy. Give me your knife.
They took mine away, but left you yours.

## RAIS

Not here ; not now ; wait !

## ASSANTU

No waiting ; P'o-l'u comes ; and first
I must make a sacrifice, a great magical device,
to be the price of my freedom from the hungry Father.
More ; those who offer boars and bulls
are safe ; but those who offer men become
then, as I will, eaters of flesh.
I never knew this before ; now
I shall need no canoe ; I shall walk safe to that shore
over the waters on the path of the blood of a man.

## THE FLAME

Without shedding of blood is no remission of sins.

99

You too know the condition.   It is known everywhere
except in the quiet green hall of P'o-l'u.

ASSANTU

Wife, why do you keep me ? quick ! the knife !
　　　　　　　　　[*He tears it from her clothing.*

THE FLAME

Life for life : but we of the Holy Ghost
know the laws of exchange better than you.
Alayu, whom you mocked, knows them better, Assantu !

ALAYU

What is he doing ?

THE FLAME

　　　　Compelling a substitution
by his own effort—fool !
　　　　　　　[ASSANTU *begins to crawl between the sleeping*
　　　　　　　　CHORUS *towards* ANTHONY.

ALAYU

　　　　　　　But what is he doing ?

THE FLAME

He thinks—saving himself from being consumed.
You were blest ; you were consumed before you knew.
Glory to the only Good who made us and bade us
all be food and all eaters of food.
Is it a wonder Christ gave you your Eucharist ?

ALAYU

He will kill Anthony !

THE FLAME

　　　　　　No.   But since you give
yourself for Anthony, it is you shall let him live.

100

Go ; whisper to Oroyo a thought in a dream,
say : ' There was no cry when the spy died.
Why ? '

> [ANTHONY *has sunk into sleep.* ASSANTU *writhes
> near him. The spirit of* ALAYU *runs and stands
> over* OROYO.

ALAYU

Oroyo, there was no cry when the spy died.
Why ?

OROYO (*in sleep*)
No cry ; that was strange.

ALAYU

Why ?

RAIS

Husband, take care. The trees are thick with sound.
Come back. Look ! my arms are empty : come.
Trees and sea and moon are thick with voices.

ALAYU

Oroyo, why was there no cry ?

OROYO (*in sleep*)
Assantu,
where was Assantu then ? why was Assantu
caught ?

ALAYU

Why, Oroyo ? wake, wake !

ASSANTU (*rising and making passes over* ANTHONY)
I give you my name, white man ! I make you me.
I prick your wrist and smear your mouth with blood

so that you speak in my blood.   I whisper to you
the tale of the images ; mine is the voice of the images
and mine their stone hand.   I am living stone,
their stone, and you are I.   Go,
away, before me, among the dead,
before me, to be consumed in my stead
by the nameless Father of terrors.

> [*He whispers in* ANTHONY'S *ear.*


ALAYU

                    No cry, Oroyo !

Why ? why ?


OROYO
Why ?

> [*He wakes.*
Where was Assantu ?


ASSANTU
In the fire in the jungle, in the running—


THE FLAME

                    See me now !

me out of the jungle, the ocean and the moon,
me the uncovenanted flame of the Holy Ghost,
me the dreadful coast across dreadful seas,
me the consuming and consumed, me in power.

> [*He runs in a circle round* ASSANTU *and* ANTHONY
>         *and comes to a stop opposite* ASSANTU, *exhibiting*
>         *himself in his glory.*

It was we whom the holy ones heard above Jerusalem
falling from the rushing flame-scattering wind
to teach the blessed the speech of heaven and us.
Can you see us ? can you hear us ? can you bear us ?

[Oroyo *catches* Assantu's *wrist from behind.* The
Flame *runs to the front of the stage.*
Oho, my people,
can you bear us ? can you hear us ? can you see us ? are
your hearts pure
to endure everywhere the speech of heaven and us ?
do you die daily and live daily in us ?
are you consumed and consuming ?—Or are you content
to get someone else to die instead of you ?
Apostates !

[*He hides himself and returns to the church.* The
Chorus *and* Anthony *start to their feet.*


Torna

Oroyo !


Siru

What is happening ?


Oroyo (*showing the knife*)
This.   Here is the spy
Tantula met ! here is P'o-l'u's man
who led our father into the snare ! our Judas
doing murder in the night.

[The Chorus *exclaim dispersedly.*
Glory to God

I woke then.


Torna

Impossible.   Why should any of us
be false. . . .


Siru

Tantula . . . P'o-l'u's men in ambush . . .
and this, . . . the knife . . . say something, Assantu.

[Assantu *remains silent, staring at* Anthony *in a
kind of ecstasy.*

103

### OROYO

And Rais ! quick, get hold of her, you women.
Tantula did not die without his sister's leave.

### SIRU

Did you know of this, Rais, and of what was meant ?

### RAIS

Do you think I shall answer you ?

### SIRU

     Treachery ! always treachery !
Alayu's fall was little beside this.
Misery of falsehood !

### OROYO

       Rais was none of us.

### SIRU

Alayu and Assantu—

### ANTHONY

     Say, that I too
was something less than you thought—but let me speak.
Those who have seen their sin know sin
and cannot be astonished.   Why this man should hate
may be strange ; that he should, cannot be.
Any temptation at any moment anywhere
may change the troth-plight : then the quality of faith
is to see, and not be abashed, and still smile.
When it knows what evil is, it is not surprised,
and till it does, it is only folly disguised.
Why did you betray the Church, brother ? . . . why
did you want to kill me ?

ASSANTU (*suddenly*)
                    I wanted a substitution.
I wanted salvation.


TORNA
But you had it ; here it is.

What more ?


ANTHONY
                    Yet tell us more.   How could I help ?


ASSANTU
Jungle-fire and jungle-blood about me !
I see the curling edge of the fire, the swirling
blood on the other shore.   The image is I ;
I am living stone.   I stand at the edge of the land,
looking across the sea to the dead shore.
My stone mouth speaks ; my stone hand
is stretched among the Christian folk and has fetched
something that something eats.   I was hungry,
I shall be hungry again.   My stone melts.
There, everywhere, a sea stained with blood
tossing up flesh, and birds wailing over me ;
O the Father, the Father, I the Father,
I walking and eating : Oy ! Oy !


TORNA
He is mad.


OROYO
Or cunning.


SIRU
                    Why does God try
his Church with all the worst evils at once ?

### RAIS

Give me my husband and let us go away.

### OROYO

P'o-l'u's men will shoot ; how will you go ?
No ; you must stay here where you chose to be.

### ANTHONY

But take him to her : let them be together.
Watch them, Oroyo.   Do you despair, Siru ?
Nonsense ; it is not as easy as that for you,
who saw in Alayu's death a mode of redemption.

### SIRU

The Church may stumble ; can the Church betray ?

### ANTHONY

Do not say so ; yet betrayal lay in the Twelve,
and Matthias took his brother's bishopric ; then
among even those first men of the new creation
there was a bishopric for him to take.   Beware
despair does not leave your own empty,
because, thinking you are someone, you become someone
to be caught by sin—and only someone so.
A nothing in God cannot despair.   I heard
a voice cry when I saw the naughting of myself
that the Faith was truer than I thought.   O truer !
A man is only himself to see himself
in his own naughting ; what one, may not all ?
See, we might have supposed the Church was good
in itself, or holy, or secure ; but now never !
It shall be a nothing and blush to hear itself named
among men or angels ; this is the burning joy
which if it has not to others it has not to God.
So to Assantu you ; so I to Alayu ;
so—O all to all and all to God !

Blessed Spirit, enlarge and charge all
with—Well, but I see I am interrupted.
The eternal Peace be with you.

THE CHORUS
And with you the Peace !
[THE MARSHAL *and* PREFECT *enter with the*
SOLDIERS.

THE MARSHAL
Sermons ?  I hope to a true and useful close,
for now you must decide—you and your people.

ANTHONY
                                        Sir,
tell us clearly on what.

THE MARSHAL
            There are two courses.
One is to take the truce I now propose,
for the sake as much of your gospel as your lives.   P'o-l'u
will undo the edicts against you ;  you shall freely teach
and practise your Rites.   If you convert us all
I promise you the Sublimity will not take it ill.
But then on your side you shall be content
to use the same Name for your god and our lord,
the fatherhood in each titled by one word.
Dogmatic explanations you may make.   We shall agree
that dogma is less important than fair living
and a free giving of exchange.   I stipulate this
because some of your sect have proved obstinate.
You will pardon the discourtesy.   Well ?

ANTHONY (*smiling*)
            And the alternative ?

THE MARSHAL

O the alternative ! I shall give you five minutes—
or less (the Prefect's men are very quick)
and then machine-guns will end everything. If
you prefer this, I will not, of course, interfere :
except so far as you yourself.


ANTHONY

I ?


THE MARSHAL

Leave that ; your answer—and pray be wise.


ANTHONY (*to* THE CHORUS)

You have heard ; we are agreed ?


THE CHORUS

Yes . . . yes.


ANTHONY

Who will give the answer ?


THE CHORUS

The Holy Ghost and you.


THE FLAME

In your voice, Anthony ; mine in yours.


ANTHONY

Thus then, always under the Church.
Sir, this dying to trespasses is a long pain,
however it be all done ; our hearts bleed
in a deed already finished—to explain this
were a riot of useless words here and to you,
who are so plausible to show us the inessential.
So. But where the potential of Christ is challenged

it becomes an act, one side death or the other.
The Church is congruous with the world and yet other,
because it has died.   There is one here now
invisible, blazing-red with shame and glory ;
she whom your men killed—Alayu, our friend.
Christ for us is only there.   I see
that at other times the Universal Church
might agree with you in its own way ; we,
if now we could take the invitation,
should agree only in yours ; it must not be.
Salvation is never, any way, a bargain ;
and if Christ must actualize himself in our death
it is we whom first he actualized in his own,
and still in his Eucharist ; if we should now twist
the Fatherhood—

THE MARSHAL
    These are fascinating metaphysics,
but my ships are waiting.   You refuse then ?

ANTHONY
                Yes.

THE MARSHAL
Very well.   You and I will talk further,
if you can speak without drink, on our way to P'o-l'u
and until the imperial cephalopods embrace you,
and you become food for the crabs, and the crabs
for the cephalopods.   Fellow, take him in charge.
Conduct him to the ships, and put him on board my own.
Three men are to guard him day and night,
unless in my personal presence.   Take him away.

ALAYU (to THE FLAME)
I am terribly afraid.

### THE FLAME

He is not ; and he
will die purposefully, as you were meant to do ;
he will die your death and you fear his fright.
This is the kingdom on earth as it is in heaven,
where this is joy—this—in him and you.
I shall meet you there.

> [*He dismisses her and she goes into the church.*

### ANTHONY

Christ in you !

### THE CHORUS

Christ in you ! Christ !
> [ANTHONY *is taken out.*

### RAIS

Lord, will you not save a man who served you ?

### THE MARSHAL

Who ? this fellow ? our dilatory spy ?
Why, what has touched him ?   I have seen such eyes
fixed in a green ecstasy of religious trance.
Assantu ! . . . His glance does not change at all.
He has fancied himself into godhead, has he not ?
The lot of such phantasts !

### RAIS

Lord, save !

### THE MARSHAL

He has swallowed himself.   If I fetched him now
out of his own grave, he would come as a child,
speechless, staring, crying.   Shall I show you ?

### RAIS

Must it be so ? cannot the magic of P'o-l'u
do better ?

THE MARSHAL (*talking slowly, his eyes fixed on* ASSANTU's)
Look, my dear Prefect !
Here you have the heightened religious mind
in its own kind, united in rapture with its god,
a paltry phenomenon, but unusual in such complete
consummation of unconsciousness else.   Our own maxim
*absorb* was his ; but the greater swallows the less,
so I him.   There is one choice everywhere—
even between us, Prefect,—and that is to be
the swallowed *or* the swallower.   I have heard say
that these Christians pretend an *and* enters—
swallow *and* be swallowed, consume *and* be consumed.
That is folly.   See, how he shakes !
A god, are you ? tell P'o-l'u you are a god ;
Ho ! the cephalopodic process could never make you
its prey !   No ; you cannot turn your eyes away.
You are falling out of your deity.
[ASSANTU *drops to the ground and dies.*
If I had time,
I would make you a barking dog at my heels, or perhaps
a stone lying on the shore ; little braggart !
If I had time . . .

RAIS
Only you have not time.
There is something you cannot rule and dare not waste ;
something, lord, that the great magic of P'o-l'u
cannot govern ; there is need now for haste ;
there is time and the end of time.


THE MARSHAL
Wise woman !
but how do you know ?—yet it is far away ;
the day can hardly be thought that will bring it near.


RAIS
It will come.

111

THE MARSHAL

When the world ends.

RAIS

That will come.

THE MARSHAL

You loved your husband then ? Well, you shall die
with him, here, among these Christians.

RAIS

Be it so.

But you *must* go now ; you *must* ; you *must*.

THE PREFECT

Excellency, she speaks truth.

THE MARSHAL

Yes. Thank you ;
but whatever time may do at last to P'o-l'u
(always officially reserving the Secluded Emperor)
there is no exchange of eating between you and me.
Do not suppose it. Yes ; I *must* go.

[*He begins to go out ; then pauses by the* SOLDIERS.

Kill her.

[*The* SOLDIERS *fire.* RAIS *falls across* ASSANTU.

Take their bodies and throw them into the sea, over the edge
yonder.

[ASSANTU *is carried out.*

He can wander there
as bodies do, to knock against a rock,
or be snapped in the belly of a shark.

[*As* RAIS *is carried by, he strikes her face.*

Hark, you,
will you tell us we *must* ? will you say there shall be an end ?
but I, you see, can send you before me to-day,
and still be at ease ; the end is so far . . .

the end of P'o-l'u . . . infinities, infinities away . . .
we cannot think it. . . .   But you, sink and be forgotten . . .

> [*He recovers himself and turns.*

The rest, Prefect, I leave to you.

> [*He salutes and goes out.*

### THE PREFECT (*calling*)

> Close in.

An end to you now, an end to your sin and salvation,
your so's and your not so's ; there is only P'o-l'u.
And you are dead.

### SIRU

> We have been dead a long while ;
all you can do is to ensure that no guile
or violence of that old unhappy life
ever stirs in us again.   Shall we not bless
you and your men and your master for such ease ?
The faster the better.   God's grace go with you,
and may his face hearten you at the end of time.

> [THE PREFECT *goes out.*

Now let us dead men sing.

### THE CHORUS

Fire of the Spirit, life of the lives of creatures,
spiral of sanctity, bond of all natures,
glow of charity, light of clarity, taste
of sweetness to sinners, be with us and hear us.

### THE FLAME

So I am ; so I do ; so I will ; and so for all.
Come !

> [*A noise of machine-gun fire.   The Christians fall.*
> I left you all to say your say :
that sometimes is the only way ; but now
I will have mine.

> [*He discloses himself and comes down.*

Rise, holy ones ; rise, confessors and martyrs !
saints, arise ! all is done ; I am here ; begun
is the gay day of our Lord ; the air of felicity
is here now, and felicitous tongues to speak.
Now no longer is the deed hidden in the promise,
but the promise laughing in the deed.   Now no need
is but of delight, and all the past
is but delight to satisfy present need.
O we do so well you cannot think ;
Well, well, and again well !   Rise.

        [THE CHORUS, *except* TORNA, *begin to stand up*.
Happy they whose first sight in heaven
is the flight or the stillness of the flames of the Holy Ghost ;
as in Jerusalem, Rome, and all the Patriarchates,
so here ; so in all the hearts who play
well their parts ; rise, blessed ones, rise !
The skies and the earth open, and there are we :
your past and future open, and there are we.

            [THE CHORUS *move round him*.
Well, well, and again well at last !
fast is our sphere fixed, and fast it moves,
all loves circling in exchange of loves.
Come !

       [*He draws them into the church ; then he returns
           towards* TORNA.
              But you, Torna, I will have you
new-called to an old life : wounds
have you, and lie near the grave,
bleeding, lonely, and not even a priest
but the least of our house ?   Yet I will settle in you
a word, as private as you must, as public as you can,
of the Holy Ghost, heard above Jerusalem ;
in you fidelity, in you magnanimity and mercy,
in you justice, in you beatitude.   Rise—
up . . . up . . . up . . .

              [*He waves* TORNA *to his feet*.

       your wounds shall heal.
You shall feel no hope ; you shall be a hope
and a witness to us between sea and sea,
to the Maker of all and the only Taker of flesh.
What, can you stand ? you see you can. On ;
forward into the jungle : faint there,
if you must, from your loss of blood. Someone soon
will come across you, and hide and feed and give
as your need may be, and you, as may be, to theirs.
These affairs are easily settled in heaven,
given on earth a single conformable mind ;
it were unkind else. Live till we come.
Our Lord will not leave himself without a witness,
and that (in the full fitness of compassion) you.
Now all begins again ; go.
You are all and you are enough ; go.
Go, and the blessing of adorable glory with you,
whom confessing the Church—hark ! everywhere
sounds—and in you ;
       [*He swings on the audience.*
    and, if you dare, in you.


   THE CHORUS (*as* TORNA *stumbles out*)
Composer of all things, light of all the risen,
key of salvation, release from the dark prison,
hope of all unions, scope of chastities, joy
in the glory, strong honour, be with us and hear us.




     FINIS